Table of Contents

EXPLORING THE PSALMS:

VOLUME 2 – EXPLORING KEY ELEMENTS

COMPILED BY HAYES PRESS

Published by:

HAYES PRESS Publisher, Resources & Media,

The Barn, Flaxlands

Royal Wootton Bassett

Swindon, SN4 8DY

United Kingdom

www.hayespress.org

CHAPTER ONE: THE ETERNAL GOD REVEALED (LINDSAY PRASHER)

———

On reading through the Book of the Psalms, one can't but be impressed with the many expressions of the appreciation of God as JEHOVAH, the timeless, ever existing One, who has revealed Himself to mankind in no uncertain way. Three aspects of this divine outgoing activity which inspired the psalmists to call upon their fellows to give praise, worship and blessing to God are 1) His Creation by the spoken Word, 2) His written Word and 3) His way of dealing with the nations. Such a God, awesomely greater than mere man, should be reverenced as such by man.

Creation

Man was the last of God's creative works and hence he was just not there when the rest of the creation was effected: so only God can tell man what happened, and he must accept it by faith. It's interesting to note what facets of creation are revealed through the psalmists by the Holy Spirit, because they concur with the first chapter of Genesis.

(i) Considerable emphasis is placed on the creation by God of the celestial orbs, which are mentioned in Psalms 19, 33 and 136. It was always necessary to remind people of this, in view of the tendency to take the sun, moon and stars as gods in their own right. In Deuteronomy

4:19, a specific warning was given to Israel against this very form of idolatry, which was widespread among the heathen.

(ii) Psalm 33:6 goes a stage further, by stating that not only did God effect the creation of the heavenly orbs, but that it was by the Word of His mouth.

(iii) Psalm 33:9 goes further still, because each phase of all creation was instantaneous with that spoken Word: "For He spake and it was done, He commanded and it stood fast". This corresponds to, "And God said ... and it was so" of Genesis 1:7, 9, 11, 14, 15, 24.

(iv) Understandably, the sun comes in for tremendous appreciation, as is so beautifully expressed by David in Psalm 19:5-6: "Which is 'as a bridegroom coming out of his chamber, And rejoiceth as a strong man to run his course. His going forth is from the end of the heaven, and his circuit unto the ends of it: And there is nothing hid from the heat thereof.

(v) The first three verses of the same psalm highlight the silent eloquence of all the celestial orbs in the praise of their creator, as day by day and night by night they go far beyond the bare minimum of their appointed purpose in "signs and seasons and days and years", by ceaselessly declaring His glory, "forever singing as they shine, the Hand that made us is divine".

The Written Word

Psalm 19 also highlights the silent eloquence of God's written Word. No audible voice declares it from heaven, but it's available to mankind, and never so freely as in today's world. The Bible is still the world's bestseller. For the psalmists, however, it was the Law of the Lord, the Old Testament Pentateuch, given by God to Moses, which was in their possession, and it was highly prized for:

- its perfection in converting the soul and giving wisdom (v.7);

- its effectiveness in bringing happiness and enlightenment (v.8);

- its truth and righteousness, promoting the fear of the Lord (v.9);

- its preciousness and sweetness (v.10);

- its reward for those who heed and keep it (v.11);

- its power to preserve lives from sinning (vv. 12-13).

Today's more extensive Old and New Testaments are equally potent in all these directions. This is particularly so, because there has appeared on earth the God-Man who was the living personification of the Law of the Lord, kept in all its perfection in every aspect. Nor did He keep it to Himself: of His disciples He said, "I have given them Thy Word".

Psalm 12 contrasts the Word of the Lord with that of mere humans, whose lives are dulled by the dross of vanity, flattery, pride and oppression of the poor. Not so our wonderful God, whose words are pure, "as silver tried in a furnace of earth, purified seven times". The psalmist complained that men who reverenced, and allowed their lives to be governed by, such words are few and far between; so it appears today.

God's action among the nations

The God who has revealed Himself in Creation and in His written Word, also expresses Himself powerfully in His dealings with the nations of the world, and the psalmists were not slow to appreciate it for the times of which they knew. A striking case was that of Egypt at Israel's deliverance from bondage, when God divided the Red Sea to allow His people's clean escape, but caused the wall of water to fall back when Pharaoh attempted to cross the Sea, drowning his mighty army, as Psalm 136: 10-15 so vividly depicts. Sihon, king of the Amorites and Og, king of Bashan equally, but less dramatically, suffered at the hand of the Lord for Israel's benefit as they moved towards the promised land. More generally, Psalm 33:16 declares that: "There is no king saved by the multitude of an host, a mighty man is not delivered by great strength."

Verse 10 of the same psalm gives warning to those who think negatively in respect of divine purpose, or just ignore it, that: "The LORD bringeth the counsel of the nations to nought: He maketh the thoughts of the peoples to be of none effect." In recent years, hasn't there been unfolding before us a vast change in world affairs. Two super-powers who formerly glared menacingly at each other, backed by enormous quantities of weapons, are now talking to each other and have actually destroyed certain of those weapons. Such barriers had to come down, because Scripture predicts that at the end time, all nations will be united against the Lord and His Anointed (Psalm 2:2). On the other hand, the grip of communism on Europe has been considerably reduced, allowing the entrance of the Word of God into countries which so recently refused its admission. This is the Lord's doing, and it is marvellous in our eyes. The Lord still rules in the kingdom of men and His divine purposes are being worked out.

Finally, Psalm 33:12 implies a longing shared by many Christians today: "Blessed is the nation whose God is the LORD". In reality, this desirable state was worked out in the past exclusively with Israel and that for short periods only. Today, there is no nation which totally takes God as the Lord: Israel certainly is far from accepting divine rule. However, the time isn't too distant when Israel will take as their Messiah the very Jesus Christ whom they once rejected and killed. That will be when He returns to earth for His millennial reign; then all nations will bow to the Lord as their God. Come soon, Lord Jesus!

CHAPTER TWO: A GOD OF SOVEREIGN MAJESTY (REG JONES)

In our meditations on the Psalms in this chapter, we will concentrate on the Sovereign Majesty of God. This is a subject which defies full description in a logical way because we as mortals can appreciate so little of the character of God, but poetry is able to achieve in measure what logical description cannot. The Psalms are full of references to God, so that in one chapter it will be impossible to cover all relevant passages. We restrict our consideration therefore to just five Psalms where the greatness of God is seen.

Psalm 29

Psalm 29 is a psalm of David in which he contemplates the voice of the Lord. His voice is described as being powerful and full of majesty. Perhaps the thunder is the best illustration we have of the power of the voice of God: although this is a natural occurrence, it is only as God controls nature that we hear thunder. God's voice is louder and more powerful than the thunder. Job exclaimed, after reviewing the wonder of God's workings, "Lo, these are but the outskirts of His ways: and how small a whisper do we hear of Him! But the thunder of His power who can understand?" (Job 26:14). How mighty the booming claps of thunder sound, but it would be a mistake for us to think that thunder is the full extent of the voice of God. As an example of how powerful God's voice can be, perhaps we might think of Elijah in Mount Horeb. There in the cave he heard the might of the Lord expressed in the wind, then in the earthquake, then in the fire but the Lord was not in these powerful natural wonders. Finally there came to him the still small voice, and the Lord was in that voice saying "What doest thou here Elijah?" (1 Kings 19:9-13).

The majesty of the Lord is seen by David in the wonders of nature - thunder, the forest fires, the earthquake, as well as in the quiet scenes of natural life - the birth of the young deer and the skipping of the calves. But all this is outshone by God's temple, where everything says Glory. "The LORD sat as King at the Flood; yea, the LORD sitteth as King for ever" (v.10), but how wonderful to contemplate that in His people the Lord exhibits His strength and He will "bless His people with peace". No matter how immense is the power of God, shown in the greatness of nature, He is much more to His people: weak and ineffectual though they might be in the earth, they have the God who works wonders on their side and His sovereign majesty, as known to them, is far beyond anything that nature is able to demonstrate.

Psalm 33

Psalm 33 is a Psalm whose author is unknown. Its first verse, however, is very much like the last verse of Psalm 32, which was a Psalm of David. Here we have more examples of the sovereign majesty of God in the wonders of His works in creation. It is not the voice of the Lord here as it was in Psalm 29, but the Word of the Lord. The distinction between voice and word is easy to appreciate. In John 12 the Father spoke from heaven declaring the glory of His Name, but not all who heard understood the message spoken. They thought it thundered. A voice can just be a sound.

The companions of Paul on the Damascus road heard the sound without understanding the message, which was for Paul's ears only.

When, therefore, we consider the references in Psalm 33 to the creation, it was "By the Word of the Lord" that the heavens were made (verse 6) and "He spake, and it was done; He commanded, and it stood fast" (v.9). We are immediately reminded of John 1:3 speaking about the Lord Jesus as the Word of God: "All things were made by Him; and without Him was not anything made that hath been made". And Hebrews 11:3: "By faith we understand that the worlds have been framed by the Word of God". No wonder that men are overawed by the great wonders of God's creation. I'm always impressed when standing on one of the high mountains of Mid Glamorgan, with a commanding view of valleys and hills beyond, by the fact that someone in authority who had a reverence for God's things has placed a plaque near to the roadside, on which are inscribed the words of Psalm 104 and verse 24, "O LORD, how manifold are Thy works! In wisdom hast Thou made them all: the earth is full of Thy riches."

Psalm 46

Psalm 46 is a psalm of the sons of Korah. They wrote such wonderful things in their psalms that we immediately respond to the sentiments which they express. The psalm is an expression of the way in which we can depend upon our God. No matter if there are earthquakes which move the mountains or tidal waves which move the seas, our God is a permanent refuge who cannot be troubled by these things. He is the author of them, so if we trust in Him, then what do we need to fear? In contrast, how serene and majestic is a mighty river where the waters flow on in a great mass with little fuss and commotion. "There is a river, the streams whereof make glad the city of God" (Psalm 46:4). Again we find that the city of God and His temple are to the fore in our consideration. Even today there are wonders of the universe which are beyond man's present ability to explore, yet the glorious One of heaven, who created all things was satisfied to live with His people in a temporary house in a desert.

Even the glorious temple of Solomon could in no way compare with the great things of God's creation, but He, the Sovereign of the Universe, who is able to choose where He dwells, elected to be with the smallest nation on earth inperhaps the least significant of lands. "God is in the midst of her; she shall not be moved: God shall help her, and that right early" (v.5). He delighted in them as they delighted in Him. Another Psalmist wished to share in this, saying in Psalm 106:4 and 5:

> "Remember me, O LORD, with the favour that Thou bearest unto Thy people; O visit me with Thy salvation: that I may see the prosperity of Thy chosen, that I may rejoice in the gladness of Thy nation, that I may glory with Thine inheritance".

Psalm 115

Psalm 115 is one of the psalms used by the people of Israel on the Passover night. It's a song of praise to the Lord and contrasts what the Lord can do in His might with the futility of idolatry. God's people must often have suffered ridicule from the nations around because their God could not be seen, a truth reflected in this psalm: "Wherefore should the nations say, Where is now their God?"

(v.2). In answer they could say "But our God is in the heavens; He hath done whatsoever He pleased". Because God is sovereign He has complete control of everything and everyone in His universe; there is no limitation to His power. Idols have mouths and cannot speak, eyes and they cannot see, hands and they cannot handle, feet and they cannot walk. Those who trust in them are going to be similarly impotent but Israel is encouraged to trust in the Lord and to praise Him. As they remembered annually the deliverance from Egypt they would rejoice in the saving power of the God who led them out from captivity and through the weary wilderness into the rich, fertile land of promise.

Psalm 93

There are many psalms which make references to the majesty of God, but one which calls for consideration particularly is Psalm 93. Another anonymous psalm, but following on from the well-known Psalm of Moses it seems as if it could quite easily fit into the same type. The poet concentrates on the majesty of the Lord seen in the things that he has made and which are visible to us all. The Lord is the King and He is clothed in majesty and girded with strength; poetic language to be sure and no exaggeration involved in it! His throne is established long, long ago and He is from everlasting. Only as God has revealed Himself will anyone be able to express these sentiments. The waters again are under review; probably because of the mighty power of the seas and the floods, perhaps known especially to the people of Israel. The Lord is above them all, and although their voice is great the Psalmist has heard the voice of God in His Word - "Thy testimonies are very sure" (v.5). For all the wonders which he has considered in his experiences in the world it is a spiritual consideration which seems to surpass all other things: "Holiness becometh Thine house, O LORD, for evermore".

Thus it is that although man may delight to understand all the wonders of nature as seen so marvellously in the world, what causes him to express most appreciation of the workings of God is His revelation of Himself to His people. So we in our day marvel at the wonders of creation, but above all we are amazed that God should reveal Himself through His Son becoming Man, and that He in serene majesty should stand before the judges of the world and never utter a word in His own defence, so that our glory may be great in His salvation (Psalm 21:5).

CHAPTER THREE: GOD THE CARING PROVIDER (KEN DRAIN)

———

God's caring provision for His people is seen from the early chapters of Genesis, epitomized in chapter 22 when the heavy-hearted Abraham told his young son, who was about to be sacrificed on the altar of obedience, that "God will provide Himself the lamb" (v.8). What a test for that great man's faith. Yet he had already seen the caring provision of God when He drew him from famine to extreme wealth and from being without children to having a son in his old age.

So it is for the believer in Christ. Peter tells us to cast all our anxiety upon Him for He cares for us. Yet still we worry. What abundant peace of mind is ours if only we would take our problems to the Lord and let Him resolve our difficulties and provide for our needs. He knows what we really need better than we do ourselves and it is the One who truly cares who appropriately provides. So often His provision is not for the needs which we see but rather those needs which He sees. And so often the needs which burden us down with worry are not the true causes of our problems. Consider the lilies of the field. Their glory is but for a day yet the Lord does not create them other than in fulness of beauty, majestic for a moment. If He cares so lovingly for the lily how much more for us?

Let us look at the caring provision of God as seen in Psalm 65. The man who is called by God and invited to dwell in His courts can expect full satisfaction for his needs. It is the eternal God of our salvation of whom the Psalmist speaks in such all-embracing terms. Indeed the breadth of His provision encompasses the globe to the uppermost parts, the oceans, the mountains, the valleys, the rivers. Nowhere is beyond God's reach.

And so the great Provider is the One who year after year prepares the ground, levelling the ridges, breaking down the hardened soil, making it receptive and yielding, providing the life-giving water and bringing up the fresh growth until the season is crowned with the fulfilment of harvest. What poetic language is used to describe the great climax of seasonal growth - the hills are girded with joy, the pastures are clothed with flocks, the valleys also are covered over with corn.

How true in our own lives that year after year the Lord works in our hearts, getting rid of the ridges of unworkable ground, the grievances, the objections, the criticisms; breaking up the soil which has been hardened by complacency, inactivity and apathy, until it is finely textured and ready for fertile use, workable in the Master's hand. He showers our lives with blessings and seeks to bring from us abundant growth. Oh, that He may look on us and see saints and assemblies which are girded with joy, clothed with flocks and covered with corn. Perhaps we may think of the joy as our heartfelt appreciation to Him, the flocks as sacrifices of praises and the corn as our spiritual food.

We see from verse 13 that provision is inextricably linked with praise. Are we so busy advising the Lord of our needs that we fail to recognize when He does provide? Let us rather respond with praise and gratitude. Let us shout for joy, and let us sing. What pleasure the Lord receives from the praise and appreciation of His people!

A recurrent theme is found in Psalm 107, repeated on four occasions, each with a different illustration of God's provision: "They cried unto the LORD in their trouble. He delivered/saved/bringeth them out of their distresses. Oh that men would praise the LORD for His goodness." Wandering in the wilderness in a desert way, the redeemed of the Lord were hungry, thirsty and fainting in their souls. Under the good hand of the Lord their wandering ceased and they were led by a straight way, their wilderness became a city of habitation and the hunger and thirst were satisfied and filled. What a joy for God's people today to be drawn from our wanderings in a spiritual desert and led into the city of habitation, God's house, where our souls are satisfied with His abundant provision. Filled with His Spirit our hunger is abated; our thirst is quenched. Do we praise the Lord for His goodness, do we thank Him, do we extol the virtues of His holy Name? Or does He wait in vain to receive thanksgiving and praise, while we act like the nine lepers who did not return to give God thanks? (Luke 17:15-17).

Those imprisoned in the dungeon, sitting in the darkness bound with chains, are brought up to the light and freedom. Those who because of their folly are unable to eat and coming to the point of death, are healed and restored. Those who experience the terror of a tempestuous sea, so graphically described in vv. 26 and 27, see the absolute stillness brought about by the calming command of the Lord. We who were enchained by sin, in spiritual darkness, have had our bands broken and have been brought to the Light of the world. Our sickness unto death has been healed and the storms of life which threatened the sin tossed soul have been calmed by the Master of ocean, and earth, and skies.

The Psalmist says "My soul thirsteth for Thee, my flesh longeth for Thee, in a dry and weary land, where no water is" (Psalm 63:1). The One who turns a wilderness into a pool of water, and a dry land into watersprings (107:35) is also the One who told the Samaritan woman at the well: "the water that I shall give him shall become in him a well of water springing up unto eternal life" (John 4:14).

Psalm 147 is filled with praise and singing to the Lord. It commences with "Praise ye the LORD" and finishes with "Praise ye the LORD". What a glorious sound to hear God's people singing His praises from hearts which are full of gratitude for the provision of His love. For the outcast, wounded in soul, broken in spirit' He gathers, heals and provides - a beautiful association of thought with the story of the good Samaritan who found the man by the roadside, bound up his wounds and took him to the inn to be cared for under protection saying, "Whatsoever thou spendest more, I ... will repay thee" (Luke 10:35).

Let no one think himself to be too insignificant to be included in the provision of the great God of heaven. The One who sees every sparrow which falls to the ground has also counted and named every star (v.4). Surely He sees us in our total dependence on Him and cares for us. The image of the clouds being prepared to distribute rain upon the earth, thus watering the grass and feeding the beast, may well be taken literally, but it also speaks beautifully of the clouds which are brought into our lives and from which the Lord dispenses the refreshing showers which bring spiritual vitality and growth. So may we see in the trials and problems which seem to hang over us the showers of blessing which He is using for our edification:

Ye fearful saints, fresh courage take;

The clouds ye so much dread

Are big with mercy, and shall break

In blessings on your head.

We are told that every cloud has a silver lining, but in the Word of God clouds are often laden with blessing. May we be saturated with His showers to bring forth fruit unto His glory.

"He filleth thee with the finest of the wheat" (v.14). How many men and women are filling themselves with the poisonous wastes of this world which satisfy for a time and then leave a greater, gnawing, hungry void! Never filling, never satisfying, this polluted bread serves only to poison and destroy, bringing us to famine conditions. What a contrast to the wholesome provision of the finest wheat which is carefully nurtured by the God of heaven to contain all that the believer needs in spiritual nutrients. "Bread of heaven, feed us now and ever more".

Men today are pre-occupied with image and presentation. The packaging of goods receives as much consideration as the contents. But to God the outward appearance, the strength of a horse, the legs of a man, are not what brings Him pleasure, but rather the condition of the heart; reverential fear and hope in His mercy. Let us examine our hearts before God as the Psalmist says, "Search me, O God, and know my heart" (Psalm 139:23).

An honest appraisal will doubtless reveal the leanness of our response to Him. The loss of spiritual appetite creates a loss of spiritual strength, leading eventually to starvation and death. How sad to realize that we can deny ourselves the very source of life. How joyous to experience the renewing energy and vitality which comes with true feeding on the Word. "Was not our heart burning within us, while He spake to us in the way" (Luke 24:32). May we grow in grace and bring forth fruit abundantly under the caring provision of our Lord.

The words in Deuteronomy 11:11-12, referring to the land promised to the enslaved Israelites, seem to encapsulate the very spirit of the three Psalms which we have considered. "But the land, whither ye go over to possess it, is a land of hills and valleys, and drinketh water of the rain of heaven: a land which the LORD thy God careth for".

God provides because He cares. He cares because He loves. What greater motivation can be found for the God of heaven to provide for us than the motivation of the love which reached its climax at the Cross of Calvary when atonement was made for our sins. And so in our salvation we see not only the forgiveness of our sins, but also a whole new relationship with a Father who cares and provides for us.

CHAPTER FOUR: THE RICHES OF GOD'S WORD (PETER HICKLING)

─────

The phrase "according unto Thy Word" occurs eleven times in Psalm 119 (RV). It emphasizes the firm basis on which the believer who trusts God stands. Every promise stands or falls because of the character of the one who makes it, and the psalmist knows that he can call on the promises that the Lord has made for life, strength, mercy and deliverance, because the Lord is true, and His Word cannot change.

Its permanence is emphasized by v.89: "For ever, O LORD, Thy Word is settled in heaven". This calls to mind Hebrews 6:13-18, which sets out the immutability of God's counsel. In this Word the psalmist is willing to place his unreserved confidence, knowing the God who has given it; such a personal faith in the Giver is essential to trust in the gift. It is obvious, of course, that confidence of this sort can only develop in one who knows what God has said; else there is nothing to trust in. We have today His Word for us in written form; the Word of God, the Bible, and there is no substitute for thorough knowledge of its precepts and its principles. Such a knowledge, to be useful, must not merely be an ability to categorize the Bible's contents, but a whole-hearted acceptance of its relevance to our lives.

Compared with its ageless wisdom and fundamental laws, the philosophies and political expedients of our time are shifting sands.

Trust in, and knowledge of' God's Word gives us a firm basis on which to ask for help from Him. The writer of the psalm could ask for God's favour (v.58), strength (v.28), lovingkindness (v.76) and deliverance (v.153) according to His Word, secure in the knowledge that what He had promised to do he was able to perform (Romans 4:21).

The source of life

Again there is a recurring phrase; the words "quicken (Thou) me" occur nine times in the Psalm. The meaning of quicken, as used in the older versions of Scripture, differs, of course, from its use in modern English, although the Oxford English Dictionary gives as the first (oldest) meaning give life to, which is the appropriate one. There is no other source of life than God; this is true both of the original giving of life and its maintenance, and in both the physical and spiritual realms. Men receive spiritual life from God by faith, and "faith comes by hearing, and hearing by the Word of God" (Rom. 10:17 NKJV). Hence the channel of life is the Word of God, and it is neglected to our disadvantage and our peril.

When we feel oppressed - "I am afflicted" (v.107) - and earthbound - "My soul cleaveth unto the dust" (v.25) - the Word of God can invigorate spiritual life, because of which we can rejoice in the Lord. When the writer rose before dawn (v.147), and knew that he would face wicked men, he hoped in the Lord's words, and looked for His life-sustaining power through them. And of course, although it may be a past experience to many of our readers, eternal life can only be obtained through faith in the Lord Jesus Christ' whose work and Person are revealed through the Scriptures.

A way of living

The "law of the LORD" (v.1) is a way to walk in; that is, a way of living. The phrase does not only refer to the Decalogue and the ceremonial law; it brings in all God's instruction to His people through His prophets. Its parallel today is what Paul called "the whole counsel of God" (Acts 20:27). The whole sum of what God has said, viewed in its proper context, is the guide for our actions; we are not at liberty to reject part. Indeed, verse 45 says that liberty lies in seeking the precepts of God - "whose service is perfect freedom". The "way" is the "trodden path" or the "marked out route"; it is marked Out by God Himself in His Word as according to His holiness, pleasing to Himself, and for the good of those who follow it. It should always be remembered that God is not a fierce martinet who imposes rules just because He wants to make things difficult for us, but the One who loves us, and cared for us so much that He gave His Son for us.

The means of cleansing

"How can a young man cleanse his way?" (v.9 NKJV) - a perennial question, for purity now is no easier or harder than it was when the psalm was written. The only way is to apply the standards of the Word. Varying human standards will lead to moral decline when society is in decline; and it is. The word hidden in the heart (v.11) is the protection against sin. The scripture refers explicitly to young men, one supposes because the temptation to and the opportunity for impurity is likely to be greatest in their case; but no-one should think that he or she cannot be tempted, whatever his age or sExodus In all cases, however, the remedy is the same, to take heed "... according to Thy Word".

The source of blessing

Obeying God's Word is a source of blessing (vv.1-2). This comes in
two ways: firstly, the commandments themselves are designed for
the good of men, so that obedience to them brings peace of mind
and harmonious relationships with others. It should be emphasized
again that God's laws are not arbitrary; He is the Maker of the
earth and everything in it, and He is better fitted than we are to
know what we should do. This presupposes that the Scriptures are
accepted as the revelation of God. Secondly, God honours those
who honour Him (1 Samuel 2:30). He is able to bless in many
ways, both spiritual and material. Paul told the Church in Ephesus
that they had been blessed "with every spiritual blessing in the
heavenly places in Christ", but we should not ignore or depreciate
material blessings, which come from Him too. Both sorts should be
valued, and accepted from the hand of God, but it would be false,
of course, to assume that because a man is rich God has made him
to prosper; the wicked sometimes prosper too!

Wisdom and understanding

The right appreciation of God's Word needs both of these.
Understanding is comprehension, the grasp of meaning, whereas
wisdom is the ability to make right judgements. "Give me
understanding" the psalmist asks five times (vv. 34, 73, 125, 144,
169), so that he can be sure that he grasps what God's will for
him is. This is not a purely intellectual grasp, however; he says
"Give me understanding, and I shall keep Thy law; yea, I shall
observe it with my whole heart" (v.34). Knowing its meaning leads
to determination to carry it out. This knowledge is the foundation
for wisdom; "Thy commandments make me wiser than mine

enemies" (v.98). The wise man has a mental armoury equipped by the Word of God, so that he is able to bring out some relevant principle to apply to every problem. The basic attitudes are still required of us; we need to know, to grasp and to apply the Word of God.

A way of thinking

The expression "mind set" is sometimes used to describe the way a person has of thinking about things. One's mind set is governed by one's education, training, environment and what one takes in. A magazine article, writing about television, says "Are you what you watch?" The answer, to a large degree, is yes. Psalm 119 refers in four places (vv. 15, 23,78,97) to meditating in the precepts, statutes and law of God Precepts are the commandments of God, the rules for life; statutes are His laws, the limits beyond which we must not go; and "law", in this sense, is the Torah, the teaching of God.

To meditate in these things is not to let the mind wander vaguely; it is to consider their implications for our own behaviour and our appreciation of the glory of God. Thus the mind set of one who meditates in the Word of God is predisposed to thinking in His way, and predisposed to reject the assumptions of the communications media and the world around. One should not feel defensive about this; no one can think from first principles about everything, and we are bound to work from some assumptions. The question is, what shall they be, those based on the authority of the Word of God, or those based on current fashion?

Truth

The bottom line of an honest man's investigation of anything is, "Is it true?" We cannot here examine all the evidence for the veracity of the Scriptures; our convictions are stated above, and we believe them to be well rounded. They certainly claim truth for themselves; v.142 says "Thy law is truth", and this was echoed by the Lord Jesus Christ Himself, when He prayed for His disciples "Sanctify them in the truth: Thy word is truth" (John 17:17). He constantly referred to the Old Testament scriptures as having the authority of the Word of God, and an attack on that belief is an attack on Him. In summary, Psalm 119 is an affirmation of belief in the Word of God as a guide to conduct and a spiritual light; that belief is still one worthy of adoption.

CHAPTER FIVE: A PROFILE OF THE GODLY MAN (J.H. JOHNSON)

———

P salm 119 gives us great encouragement because the psalmist was, like ourselves, a man very conscious of failure. Yet he was a godly man. Some think the writer was Daniel. A godly man is not perfect in the sense of being sinless, neither is he a sinner in the sense of being deliberately so. We select only a few verses out of the 176 in the psalm for this profile of the godly man.

Desire for Reviving

He was often cast down in spirit because he was so conscious of the strength of his fleshly nature, as are all men and women of faith, and cried to God, "My soul cleaveth unto the dust" (v.25). He remembered the day when he experienced the quickening power of the Word of God, "This is my comfort in my affliction: for Thy Word hath quickened me" (v.50). He was born of the Spirit and became aware of the corruption of the old nature, and because of that there arise to God repeatedly those supplicating cries, "Quicken Thou me". We, too, know the cry "Quicken me". How important to be right with God. We all want revival, but it starts with ME. O God, revive me! Make me to live.

Paul knew the experience of being cast down perhaps in greater measure than any of us, "O wretched man that I am! Who shall deliver me out of the body of this death?" He answers his own question in a glad assurance begotten of the Spirit of God, "I thank God through Jesus Christ our Lord" (Romans 7:24-25). We take comfort and press on in the knowledge that godly men and women have uttered the same yearning cries.

Cleansing by the Word

"Wherewithal shall a young man cleanse his way?" The psalmist answers his own question: "By taking heed thereto (i.e. to his way) according to Thy Word" (v.9). The Word of God has a cleansing effect on our lives. Peter says to obedient disciples, "Ye have purified your souls in your obedience to the truth unto unfeigned love of the brethren". Because "to step aside is human" God has provided that when we sin, "if we confess our sins, He is faithful and righteous to forgive us our sins, and to cleanse us from all unrighteousness" (1 John 1:9). How wonderful! And "how rich the precious blood once spilt"! The writer of the psalm knew that there is a rich blessing for those "who walk in the Law of the Lord ... that seek Him with the whole heart. Yea, they do no unrighteousness ... that is, not habitually. They walk in His ways" (it is, their habit of life). The psalmist longed, "Oh that my ways were established to observe Thy statutes! Then shall I not be ashamed when I have respect unto all Thy commandments" (vv. 1-6).

His Love for God's Word

The Word of God was everything to the psalmist. "The Law of Thy mouth is better to me than thousands of gold and silver" (v.72). "How sweet are Thy words unto my taste! Yea, sweeter than honey to my mouth!" (v.103). "Thy Word have I laid up in mine heart, that I might not sin against Thee".

How full of contradictions the Scriptures seem to the natural man! Yet to the man of God there are no contradictions. Like Isaiah and Peter the psalmist had times when he was so conscious of the holiness of God that he exclaimed; "My flesh trembleth for fear of Thee' and I am afraid of Thy judgements" (v.120). As he viewed the inequities and evils of this life he cried out to God, "My soul breaketh for the longing that it hath unto Thy judgements at all times" (v.20). How true and compatible also are the statements, "I rejoice at Thy Word, as one that findeth great spoil" (v.162) and "My heart standeth in awe of Thy words" (v.161).

Even those who are not great students have times in their daily reading of Scripture when their heart rejoices as if God has spoken personally to them. Also there are portions that cause us to experience joy, reverence and awe for God and His Word. That the infinitely holy God should so love a world of sinners like you and me that He gave His only Begotten Son to suffer for our sins on the Cross of Calvary, is most awesome; and that whosoever believes on Him should not perish but have eternal life is most joyous. Consider again, "My heart standeth in awe of Thy words". Do we today "stand in awe" of the words of God? Have we lost something of the love, reverence and awe that we ought to have for the Word of God?

The heart of the Godly Man

The heart of this man of God reveals his spiritual stature. How high do we reach when standing alongside him? "My soul breaketh for the longing that it hath unto Thy judgements at all times" (v.20) and "I have longed for Thy salvation, O LORD; and Thy Law is my delight" (v.174). Many of us can relate to the second, but few of us to the first of these heart longings.

"Mine eyes run down with rivers of water, because they observe not Thy Law (v.136). Surely he is referring to some of God's ancient people. How like tenderhearted Jeremiah, "Mine eye shall weep sore, and run down with tears, because the LORD's flock is taken captive" (Jeremiah 13:17). We remember how the Lord Himself wept over Jerusalem, because its people knew not the time of their visitation. Paul, too, had a heart like his Master. "I have great sorrow and unceasing pain in my heart. For I could wish that I myself were anathema from Christ for my brethren's sake, my kinsmen according to the flesh" (Rom. 9:1-3).

The godly minister, John Welsh, lived in Scotland over 300 years ago. On one occasion, shortly after retiring for the night, he rose up and went to another room. His wife, a considerable time later, went to see why he was absent so long and found him weeping and praying. She remonstrated with him. "Woman", he replied in the custom of his times, "I am responsible for more than 300 souls and I know not how it is with many of them". Do we have such tender hearts?

The godly man however was not a weeping weakling who lacked strength of purpose. The psalmist had known times when the going got tough. "The proud have had me greatly in derision: yet have I not swerved from Thy Law" (v.51). Again, "They had almost consumed me upon earth; but I forsook not Thy precepts" (v.87). He drew his strength from God; he knew, as we do, that the arm of flesh will fail and prayed, "Strengthen Thou me", assured that the faithful God (v.90) would do in the present as He had done in the past. These and other verses show that he had purposed in his heart to serve God according to His Word, cost what it may. Like the Lord he was steadfastly minded to do the will of God.

His Habit of Meditation

Meditation is something that all of us can do. Much study is a weariness of the flesh, but meditation can be engaged in throughout the day. The Hebrew word used in Psalm 119 is not the word used in Joshua 1:8 or Psalm 1:2 (which has the thought of murmuring in pleasure) but a word which according to Dr. Strong means "to ponder i.e. (by implication) converse ..." Seven times the psalmist uses this verb. He speaks of meditating in "Thy precepts", "Thy statutes", "Thy Word", "Thy wondrous works" and "Thy Law is my meditation all the day". During the day he turned over in his mind some portion of the Word. "Thy testimonies ... are my counsellors (RV margin, the men of my counsel)" (v.24).

Knowing God and His Word

He prayed "Open Thou mine eyes, that I may behold wondrous things out of Thy Law", for he is conscious of hidden depths in the Word of God and his need of spiritual insight. He also knew that "the opening (KJV: entrance) of Thy words giveth light; It gives understanding to the simple". How glad the two on the road to Emmaus were, how their heart burned within them, while He spoke to them in the way, while He opened to them the Scriptures. And on our pilgrim journey we, too, can have like experiences.

Exchanging thoughts of God and His Word with godly companions can be very enriching, and so the psalmist says, "I am a companion of all them that fear Thee, and of them that observe Thy precepts" (v.63). He knew the need for separation from the "proud that are cursed, which do wander from Thy commandments" (v.21). Like his companions he confesses, "I am a sojourner in the earth" (v.19). Because he was godly he suffered persecution from the men of this world and sometimes wondered how long he could stand it: "How many are the days of Thy servant? When wilt Thou execute judgement on them that persecute me?" He rejoiced in the knowledge that, "The LORD is my portion" (v.57), and therefore he gladly declared with upturned face to God, "Thy statutes have been my songs in the house of my pilgrimage". Many of us who are not great singers know times when a song of praise and thanksgiving rises from our hearts and we spontaneously "sing" to "the Lord of all" (even if slightly off tune); how we wish we could sing with all our being - like the skylark!

Confidence in God

"Thou art good, and doest good" (v.68). "I know, O LORD, that Thy judgements are righteous, and that in faithfulness Thou hast afflicted me" (v.75). This is the language of the men and women of faith in God of all ages who also individually say, "I am Thine, save me" (v.94), and "Thou art my Hiding Place and my Shield" (v.114), and earnestly desiring spiritual health, pray, "Make Thy face to shine upon Thy servant" (v.135).

CHAPTER SIX: A PILGRIM NATION (BRIAN FULLARTON)

———

P salms (Hebrew: Tehillim) means "Praises". The four psalms under consideration are a praising of the Lord for His wondrous works, wonders of old, judgements of His mouth and everlasting mercy. These sacred songs reveal the Lord in history, teaching and prophecy. The history of God's dealings with Israel afford hope to the people of God today.

The sanctuary deliberations of the Triune God and the outworking of these counsels for a pilgrim nation in the appointment of a law (Psalm 78:5) are described principally in the book of Exodus. They are expanded in Leviticus and provide insights into the divine perspective on events in Psalms 77 and 78. The books of Numbers and Deuteronomy provide the backcloth to Psalms 105 and 106 which mainly have relevance to "the Land" (vv. 11 and 24 respectively). Many of the incidents occur in all four psalms. A breakdown of the main historical points may be helpful:

- Covenant with Abraham - Genesis12 & 22; Psalm 105
- Joseph – Genesis 37; Psalm 105
- Israel in Egypt:
- Early days – Exodus 1; Psalm 105
- Wonders & signs – Exodus 7-12; Psalm 77,78,105,106
- Red Sea – Exodus 13-15; Psalm 77,78,106
- Waters of Marah – Exodus 15; Psalm 78
- Manna - Exodus 16; Psalm 78,105,106

- Massah and Meribah – Exodus 17; Psalm 78,105,106
- Sinai - Exodus 19; Psalm 77,78,105
- Molten Calf - Exodus 32; Psalm 106
- Korah and company – Numbers 16; Psalm 106
- Baal-peor – Numbers 25; Psalm 106

Israel's experiences are our lessons - "For whatsoever things were written aforetime were written for our learning" (Romans 15:4). This nation, a people called and redeemed of God, was unique. Israel had a divine deliverer and guide who always remained "the same" (cf. Malachi 3:6, Hebrews 13:8). He was immutable in His purpose for this pilgrim nation, infallible in His word to them and inexhaustible in His resources for them. His works on their behalf are seen in the history of the nation; His ways were only to be detected and appreciated by submission to His will. He is, as seen in these psalms, the God of power and love, patience and hope. Attributes such as these are presented again and again.

Days of old, years of ancient times must be considered and examined (Psalm 77:5). The deeds of the Lord are so different from the works of men; they are wonderful (vv. 11-14), none more so than the redemption of a people by the invincible power of His hand from defeat, disaster and even death. Redemption brings relationship.

Through God's mighty salvation from Egypt and later at the Red Sea they were to become sons and daughters of God. Through obedience to His Word they would be constituted His nation (Exodus 19:5,6). Salvation was to lead to service. "I AM" exercised His initiative and prerogative to have a people to serve Him - I will bring you out (Exodus 6:6); I will take you to Me (Exodus

6:7); I will bring you in (Exodus 6:8). That purpose for a pilgrim people was planned in heaven and executed on earth. They were special and unique, their pilgrim status ordained of God. They were divinely purchased, separated and called together. The God who delivered them received them as "His own"; this experience is comparable to the promises of 2 Corinthians 6:16-18. Leadership was entrusted to a prophet and a priest - Moses and Aaron (Psalm 77:20), thus their care and well-being rested in divinely appointed shepherds (see Acts 20:28). God's favour and mercy never wavered throughout all their changing attitudes and responses to His will.

A brief synopsis of some of Israel's experiences reveal that God's works are not only to be remembered, but transmitted to others (Psalm 78:4,7), the things heard ... the same commit... to teach others (2 Timothy 2:2). His praises and strength were to be celebrated in song.

The great covenant sworn to Abraham goes right back to Genesis 12:2. One man called by divine grace is to become one nation, one people. Abraham was a separated man; his spiritual progeny were to be the same. Men of stature come to prominence in Psalm 105, all found in the book of Moses. These are His anointed: Abraham, Isaac, Jacob, Joseph, Moses and Aaron. These were men of the nation, pilgrims who lived for and among the people of God. Sent by Him, they sojourned and served Him well (vv. 17 and 23). Most remarkable of all is Joseph's experience in the dungeon, "His soul entered into the iron" (v.18 RVM). The nation's elevation came through the sufferings of the saviour Joseph; more than his flesh, his very being knew the bitterest of pain. Such words point on to the Saviour whose suffering was far greater than Joseph's, as borne out by the words of Isaiah 53:12: "He poured out His soul unto death". Joseph's soul entered into suffering, the Lord Jesus' soul was poured out as a result of it.

The great miracle-working power of God fills the pages of Exodus as it does these psalms. From Egypt to Canaan, from the field of Zoan to the Mount Zion His wonders unfold (Psalm 78:12,54,68). Two sentences in Psalm 77 suffice to cover Exodus chapters 7-12. The plagues which were in fact signs are well enumerated in verses 44-51 of Psalm 78. Rivers, fields, vineyards, trees, cattle and the prime of Egypt's youth fell into the path of God's righteous anger. They were not spared. In contrast Israel went out full, from slavery to service, from oppression to God's presence, from the valley of despair to the mountain of His holiness (v.54). Materially prosperous, spiritually strong Israel fled Egypt. If they had remained they could not have enjoyed the sweetness of their pilgrim character. The world detests separated people who are different from its ways and disinterested as to its pursuits. Psalm 105 again bears out the evidence of God's grace in Egypt in the opportunity of repentance before His outbreak of judgement. Egypt thought it could play with God, tamper with spiritual issues and disregard His warnings.

The Red Sea epic is the incident most widely covered, although without mention in Psalm 105. He who commanded the earth into being had no difficulty commanding the sea to rise and remain erect while His called ones passed through. The fascinating account of Israel's deliverance here conveys the truth of baptism - death, burial and resurrection to walk in newness of life (1 Corinthians 10:2; Romans 6:4). Egypt's hosts, the enemies of God's people, were swept away by the Lord's band causing the waters to return. No single component of the enemy force survived. Other nations have endeavoured to effect a holocaust policy - to no avail (e.g. Revelation 20:9). So, the force that destroyed the Egyptians saved the Israelites - the water. Their way of life was changed. They were now free to serve, redeemed from a vain and monotonous way of life (cp. 1 Peter 1:18). The song of jubilation at the Red Sea is beautifully echoed (Exodus 15:11; Psalm 77:13-14). The day-pillar of cloud and the night-pillar of fire assured this despised and pilgrim people of the Lord's watchfulness and protection.

The Manna (Exodus 16) was the heavenly bread, the' food of angels. It was sent in bountiful supply, typical of the true, living, heavenly and life-giving Bread of God, the Lord Jesus, who would later come to an ungrateful nation (John 6:32-33, 35). Bread in the morning, choice fowl in the evening, fresh food supplied each day with the exception of the sabbath; for forty years this was their staple diet. They were as a nation separate even in their eating habits, yet they quickly became unthankful and critical. God's judgement descended and the place names were called burning and burying (Taberah and Kibroth-Hattaavah Numbers 11:1 and 34). When redemption is forgotten, stubbornness, scepticism and provocation follow; faith and love quickly disappear (Hebrews 2:3).

Massab and Meribah (Exodus 17 and Numbers 20) provide the setting for verses 15 and 16 of Psalm 78. Their haranguing of the servant of the Lord betrayed their short memory and constant dissatisfaction with the Lord. Moses was denied entrance into "the Land" because of his reaction to the people's perpetual disenchantment. They spoke against God (Psalm 78:19), believed not His Word, trusted not His power.

We move on to Sinai (Psalm 77:17, 18 etc.) where the people were to meet God. The Lord is not a distant force, a remote ruler. They were His flock one visible unity; the seed of Abraham - separated; the children of Jacob chosen. Their nationhood was constituted by covenant, command, oath and statute and their obedience was expected (Exodus 19:4-5). For a people to be formed, governed and functional, there had to be clear law and the teaching of it. They were collectively favoured and individually blessed, remembered by the Lord and visited with His great salvation (Psalm 106:4): a race prospered by God, a nation rejoicing in God, an inheritance chosen by God. Yet they became inconsiderate and disobedient.

Other incidents we summarize briefly:

- Exodus 32 - The molten calf - false worship and summary judgement - 3,000 slain.
- Numbers 14 - Despising the gospel of the Land - those brought out of Egypt died in the wilderness over half a million.
- Numbers 16 - Korah and company - Envy and malice against leadership about 300 perished.
- Numbers 25 - Whoredom at Baal-Peor - demon worship and sacrificing to the dead and fornication with the Moabites 24,000 fatally smitten.

So, we find sad notes as well as joyful strains throughout these psalms. God's greatness remains unchanged; He is eternal; praise is rightly His. "And let all the people say, Amen".

CHAPTER SEVEN: IN THE PROMISED LAND (DAVID WEBSTER)

───

U nder the leadership of the faithful warrior Joshua, Israel entered and began to subdue the land promised to them by God. This was the culmination of a series of events overruled by the mighty hand of God going back to the time Abraham received His promise (1). Despite the long interval in terms of human history, the process was given fresh impetus when God delivered His people from Egypt, entered into a covenant relationship with them and brought them through forty years of wandering in the desert "to the border of His holy land" (Psalm 78:54).

Three of the Psalms included in this study (Psalms 78, 105 and 106) are an historical survey of the attitude of a great God to His people and of the response of that people to their God. The fourth (Psalm 133) presents the ideal and a challenge. The references in brackets refer to these four Psalms.

Early Failure (78:56-64; 106: 34-39)

They hardly had long enough to settle down and have a good look at the land before "they put God to the test and rebelled" - straight disobedience in that "They did not destroy the peoples as the Lord had commanded them" (106:34). They preferred to mingle with them rather than maintain their separation and in worshipping their idols they soon became as debased as the Canaanites were.

R.K. Harrison comments about the Canaanite religion "that its sordid and debased nature stood in marked contrast to the high ethical ideals of Israel. The absolute lack of moral character in the Canaanite deities made such corrupt practices as ritual prostitution, child sacrifice, and licentious worship the normal expression of religious devotion and fervour" (2) and that was what the people of God found so attractive! The Psalmist calls it a snare, the book of Judges provides the historical details. Even Moses had solemnly warned them about it in his final address to the people, yet they "rebelled against the Most High", they were so "disloyal and faithless ... they aroused His jealousy with their idols" (78:57-58).

In a society so very different in detail, yet as morally bankrupt and as displeasing to God as that of the Canaanites of old, the people of God today need to be careful what they find attractive. John's injunction (3) reminds us that it is still God's will that His people today maintain their separation from the world, and Paul commands us to "have nothing to do with the fruitless deeds of darkness" (4). If "the LORD was angry with His people and abhorred His inheritance" (106:40) in those days, what will His attitude be to us now?

God's Work On Their Behalf (78:54-55; 105:44)

It is a sobering thought that, within a generation from the time of Joshua's death and the elders who were his contemporaries, an Israelite in the promised land would have been able to survey a society very different from what God intended (5). He would have seen a society sunk in corruption, ravaged by the sword (78:62), distressed (106:44), intimidated by their foes (106:41) to such an extent that normal social life almost ceased in Israel (78:63). They were obsessed with high places (78:57) and the custom of the nations (106:35), hamstrung by their rebellion (78:56) and defection, spiritually bewildered, ensnared by the idols they worshipped (106:36). Worst of all, they were defiled by the totality of their evil actions (106:33) and as a consequence rejected by the God who had "brought out His people with rejoicing" (105:43) and had made them heir to the lands, houses and similar assets of others.

No blame for this pitiful state of spiritual bankruptcy could be charged to Israel's God. Every circumstance had been provided for, and they entered the land armed with a wealth of experiences to sustain them and promises to take hold of. In shepherd-like terms God is described as bringing them to the land and allocating them the pleasant places, driving the enemy away. Settled in towns they had not built, and living in houses they had not had to work for, they were indeed a privileged people. The Psalmist realized that the land was not simply a convenient place to settle but that it was their inheritance, something given to them by their God to keep and treasure and which was intended to bring them great blessing.

A Lesson Not Learned (106:40-43)

"Again the Israelites did evil in the eyes of the LORD" (6). That repeated lament of Israel's sin from the book of Judges contrasts with "Many times He delivered them" of Psalm 106. "The period was a pendulum of punishment and reprieve" (7) testifying to the folly of the people and the greatness of the love and mercy of their God. It is good that we have a merciful God, but bad if we take advantage of such kindness. "Shall we go on sinning", asks Paul, "so that grace may increase? By no means!" (8). Unlike the Israelites who "were bent on rebellion" (106:43) we must make it our aim to be "holy and pleasing to God" (9). But what was it they were doing? Simply trying their best to fit in and be like all the other nations! And this was the very thing that was forbidden to them! Unfair? Rather it was for their spiritual health as well as God's honour.

One author puts it like this: Yahweh knew that copying the ways of the nations would disfigure His people's worship and lifestyle. It would blunt their effectiveness as His instrument in history. And it would change their nature. By becoming like the nations, His people would no longer be like Him. They would have lost their holiness (10). This applies equally to the people of God today and we must strive against it. This will surely cost us something in time and effort, simply reading about it will not do!

A God who Takes Notice (78:65-67; 106: 44-48)

Although judgement follows disobedience, God is never indifferent to His people's distress. In Psalm 78 the analogy is with a man awakening from sleep or from intoxication and exercising his strength once again. Perhaps that's how it looked from the human perspective. Psalm 106 looks at it from God's side: He took note; He heard; He remembered; He relented! Crying to God coupled with true repentance brings divine power to His people. We should never be slow to confess our failings and ask for forgiveness, nor should we be reluctant to cry out to the God who is able to deliver us when we are in trouble.

A Spiritual Peak (78:68-72; 133:1-3)

Reality constrains the Psalmist to confess "We have sinned" (106:6) and to relate the sad history of Israel's failure. Yet there is cause for rejoicing and praise. Psalm 78 concludes on a high note: God's purposes are not frustrated by anything His people do. God is sovereign and remains in control. He rejects and He chooses. Judah becomes the honoured tribe into whose territory the ark was entrusted after its return from the Philistines, and where in Jerusalem "Mount Zion which He loved" (78:68) was situated and from where David ruled as a man after God's own heart (11), bringing Israel to a spiritual peak not to be repeated until our Lord Jesus comes to reign.

That united kingdom over which David ruled was to be a "good and pleasant" place to dwell in. The people were to enjoy the fellowship described by David in Psalm 133. Unity is precious to God because it is a witness to the character of God. Unity is seen in the people coming to God on His terms and in obedience. Like the consecrating oil that flowed down from the head of the High Priest consecrating him entirely or the mountain dew that makes the whole of Hermon fruitful, so is unity based on allegiance to the Lord and it produces the conditions where the Lord can bestow blessing.

Obligations and Privileges (78, 105, 106)

Psalm 78 opens with an invitation to pay attention to God's law, emphasizing the importance of teaching or doctrine to the people of God. As the historical review clearly shows, it is not good enough to be in the land and numbered among God's people if no attention is paid to the detailed directions for daily life or to the divine demarcation between acceptable and unacceptable behaviour. It also stresses the obligation to pass these truths on to subsequent generations together with "the praiseworthy deeds of the LORD, His power, and the wonders He has done" (78:4).

In Psalm 105 it is the nations outside of Israel who are to be told about the greatness of God, a vision of outreach, while the people of God, in an attitude of worship, sing praises, glory in His name and rejoice. We should examine ourselves today: how effectively are we telling the peoples about our great God? How eager are we to sing praises and rejoice? It is a Psalm which overlooks the failure and rebellion and reminds us of how God sees us in Christ. By way of contrast Psalm 106 does go into such detail yet its climax testifies to the value in returning to the Lord and to His willingness to respond to our cries of "Save us" (106:47).

The people responded with an "Amen". Sadly such spiritual appreciation so often seemed to be short-lived. By the time many generations had passed and the Lord Himself walked among His people, their own traditions had taken precedence over God's law and those outside of themselves were regarded with disdain (12). It is a solemn lesson to the people of God at the end of the twentieth century.

All references are from the New International Version: (1) Genesis 17:8. (2) Old Testament Times IVP. (3) 1 John 2:15-17. (4) Ephesians 5:11 (5) See Judges 3:7-14. (6) See Judges 3:12, 6:1, etc. (7) L.C. Allen, The Psalms, The International Bible Commentary (8) Romans 6:1. (9) Romans 12:1 (10) Alan Kreider, Journey Towards Holiness, Marshall Pickering (11) See 1 Samuel 13:14 (12) See John 8:48

CHAPTER EIGHT: GOD'S PROTECTION AND DELIVERANCE (LEONARD ROSS)

———

G od is "a God of deliverances" (Psalm 68:20), and many of His servants have proved this by experience. Daniel's three companions are typical. With godly boldness they answered Nebuchadnezzar "our God whom we serve is able to deliver us from the burning fiery furnace; and He will deliver us out of thine hand, O king" (Daniel 3:17). That chapter ends with Nebuchadnezzar declaring, "there is no other god that is able to deliver after this sort". Paul speaks of the God who delivered him in the past out of a great death, who would also deliver him in present and future experiences (see 2 Corinthians 1:10). David in the 18th Psalm - a Psalm of deliverance rejoiced in the mystery that God "delivered me because He delighted in me" (v.19). We continue our meditation on this aspect of God's character through the doors of Psalm 121.

I will lift up mine eyes unto the mountains: from whence shall my help come? My help cometh from the LORD, which made heaven and earth (vv.1,2). These are not the eyes of the sightseer. Here is a pilgrim disciple who feels his need. The mountains which he sees in reality or by recollection are but a token of the One who is beyond them, for even "the mountains shall depart, and the hills be removed" (Isaiah 54:10), but "before the mountains were brought forth ... Thou art God" (Psalm 90:2). The attitude of many today is just the same as recorded in Psalm 3:2, "Many there he which say of my soul, There is no help for him in God". The taunt of the nations was "Where is now their God?" (Psalm 115:2). The following verse gives the answer: "our God is in the heavens". And it is to this God (not the heavens or the hills) that the psalmist looks for help, to the God who "made heaven and earth" (Psalm 146:6).

Psalm 34 is a lesson from experience from one who was tempted and afflicted. To the onlooker, David was a madman (1 Samuel 21), and from that account it would seem that the fear of man had become a snare - no help for him in God! But the Psalm reveals his soul. David was in a desperate situation, but underneath were the everlasting arms of a God who is ever the refuge and strength of His own, a very present help in trouble. It is commendable, but should not really be surprising, if in the midst of trials we see the exercise of faith and trust in such a God, and not a display of fear even though "the mountains be moved the mountains shake". David recalls, "I sought the LORD, and He answered me, and delivered me from all my fears" (Psalm 34:4).

Our lives as Christians are not lived in isolation - no man lives to himself or dies to himself (Romans 14:7) - and David's experience affected others. Just as he looked to the Lord and was delivered, so his companions "looked unto Him, and were lightened: and their faces shall never be confounded" (Psalm 34:5). "Many are the afflictions of the righteous, but the LORD delivereth him out of them all" (v.19), and as Peter said, it is only the Lord who knows how to deliver the godly out of temptation (2 Peter 2:9). This deliverance can be a testimony to others who may have said, "There is no help for him in God".

He will not suffer thy foot to be moved: He that keepeth thee will not slumber. Behold, He that keepeth Israel shall neither slumber nor sleep. The LORD is thy keeper (vv.3-5). "The LORD is thy keeper" is the delightful theme of the Psalm, and the Lord was to David, in every way, his "keeper", his "protector". In that 34th Psalm already referred to, he declares that "the angel of the LORD encampeth round about them that fear Him, and delivereth them" (v.7). Unseen guardian perhaps, but there. We also can be thankful for the care of those "ministering spirits, sent forth to do service" (Hebrews 1:14).

"He will not suffer thy foot to be moved". It is God's desire that His disciples be unshakeable, or as Paul puts it, "stedfast, unmoveable, always abounding in the work of the Lord" (1 Corinthians 15:58). But there is much to distract us from this ideal. In Psalm 94, the psalmist considers the success of the wicked, the workers of iniquity. "How long" he cries, "shall the wicked triumph?" They were a sore trial to him! The wicked assume that the Lord will not see (Psalm 94:7) and they continue headlong in what is really a path of self-destruction, even though it has all the appearance of every prosperity. A consideration of this Psalm, and also, for example, Psalm 73, leads us to conclude that it is dangerous to equate material prosperity with spiritual blessing. Yet, too often, there is a deep, sometimes hidden, desire in our lives to possess - the danger is that desire develops into covetousness. The psalmist confesses in Psalm 73 "as for me, my feet were almost gone; my steps had well nigh slipped ... when I saw the prosperity of the wicked". A similar condition is revealed in Psalm 94 - "my foot slippeth" (v.18). But we are now considering that the Lord is the keeper of His own, the One who will not suffer their foot to be moved! So it required a visit to the sanctuary, and it was there in the presence of the Lord that true values were regained (Psalm 73:17). It was at the moment that the psalmist said "my foot slippeth" that the mercy of God upheld him (Psalm 94:18).

The God of the psalmist was One who does not even slumber, far less sleep, and so it was with confidence that David said in Psalms 3 and 4, "I laid me down and slept; I awaked; for the LORD sustaineth me" and "In peace will I both lay me down and sleep: for Thou, LORD, alone makest me dwell in safety". There is evidence here of a child-like faith and confidence to which we do well to aspire. Do we really believe that there is a faithful One watching over every moment of our lives, guarding, protecting, delivering from foes seen and unseen? The confident message of the Psalms is that there is. "The LORD is thy shade upon thy right hand. The sun shall not smite thee by day, nor the moon by night" (vv.5-6).

Yes, He is the day and night God! His protection is complete, and this is reflected in Psalm 61 which perhaps refers to a time when David was unable to be physically present at the place of God's dwelling - he may have been in exile. But God "is not far from each one of us" (Acts 17:27). His heart was overwhelmed and though he seemed "at the end of the earth", his God was not inaccessible. Indeed in verse 4 he says "I will dwell in Thy tabernacle for ever: I will take refuge in the covert of Thy wings". Where is this refuge? Surely no less a place than the Mercy Seat, the very heart of God's dwelling, in the very presence of God. David lived there in spirit. The present dispensation equivalent is the Throne of Grace of Hebrews 4:16, the place to which with boldness, the people of God may come to receive mercy and find grace to help in a time of need. It's ever a day of much need, and much need therefore for each of us to be living in spirit in the very presence of God seeking, as Colossians 3 encourages, "the things that are above, where Christ is, seated on the right hand of God". The One who today is at the right hand of the Majesty in the heavens, is the same who is our shade at our right hand He is no distant Deliverer!

Psalm 142 records David's experience in the cave - it is the cry of a man in distress. There is no cave, however, which is so deep that it smothers the disciple's cry to his God. As in Psalm 61, David's spirit is overwhelmed within him, and there was no one at his right hand. "Look on my right hand, and see; for there is no man that knoweth me: refuge hath failed me; no man careth for my soul" (Psalm 142:4). For David, the cave was a place of learning and proving that while earthly friends may sometimes fail "there is a friend (lover) that sticketh closer than a brother". The Lord was at his right hand to be his shelter, "For He shall stand at the right hand of the needy, to save him from them that judge his soul" (Psalm 109:31).

"No man careth for my soul bring my soul Out of prison" he cries in verses 4 and 7, and this leads us to consider: "The LORD shall keep thee from all evil; He shall keep thy soul" (v.7). There is nothing more vital than the soul. If it is kept, then all is safe. This isn't to say that the disciple will never encounter difficulties or problems or will never face trials as a result of his faith. He isn't cocooned from adversity. Indeed the whole path of the faithful disciple is a taking up of his cross. What is promised, however, is a constant and protective Presence, to enable him to cope. This verse of Psalm 121 finds a delightful fulfilment in John 17 where the Lord Jesus prays for His disciples, "Holy Father, keep them in Thy Name ... while I was with them, I kept them in Thy Name which Thou hast given Me: and I guarded them, and not one of them perished ... I pray not that Thou shouldest take them from the world, but that Thou shouldest keep them from the evil one" (vv. 11-15). Blessed Master!

They all would say like Peter "I will not deny Thee", yet they all would be found sleeping while He prayed - they all would desert Him and flee - Peter would deny Him. Yet their souls were kept, and preserved through these experiences to serve Him in faithfulness. "The LORD shall keep thy going out and thy coming in, from this time forth and for evermore" (v.8). "This time" is like the "today" of Hebrews 3 and we are assured that the protective care of God continues on for as long as we need to be kept. And so we say with David "Blessed be the Lord, who daily beareth our burden, even the God who is our salvation (Selah). GOD IS UNTO US A GOD OF DELIVERANCES" (Psalm 68:19-20).

CHAPTER NINE: GOD'S CHOSEN REJECTED (GREG NEELY)

———

Peter writes about the Lord Jesus Christ that He was "rejected by men, but choice and precious in the sight of God ... the stone which the builders rejected, this became the very corner stone" (1 Peter 2:4,7).

What a sad commentary on men, that even as they looked for their Messiah to come, when He appeared, they refused to accept Him. They wanted a majestic king; they got a servant King whom they did not know and did not receive. "He was in the world, and the world was made through Him, and the world did not know Him. He came to His own, and those who were His own did not receive Him" (John 1:10-11). What marvellous grace that "as many as received Him, to them He gave the right to become children of God, even to those who believe in His Name" (John 1:12). He is God's Son, God's Chosen; and men rejected Him, their eyes blinded by sin and self-righteousness.

Psalm 1 describes the man who is blessed, or abundantly happy, as one who "does not walk in the counsel of the wicked, nor stand in the path of sinners, nor sit in the seat of scoffers!" Instead, he finds his delight in the law of the Lord, and he meditates in it day and night. While we can learn lessons ourselves from this, it appropriately describes the character of the Lord Jesus, who said of Himself to His Jewish followers: "Do not think that I came to abolish the Law or the Prophets; I did not come to abolish, but to fulfil" (Matthew 5:17). His delight was in the law of the Lord. Indeed, He was the fulfilment of it! The counsel of His God was where He walked, and the path of His Father was where He stood. He said of Himself, "for I always do the things that are pleasing to Him" (John 8:29). It is evident from His life, His actions, His words, that His delight, His treasure, was with His Father.

David is the man of Psalm 40 who lovingly tells his God: "I delight to do Thy will, O my God; Thy Law is within my heart" (v.8). The writer to the Hebrews takes up the theme in chapter 10:5-10 and points out that this more fully describes the Lord and His delight in the things of His God. Those sacrifices and offerings that the Law required became odious to the Lord as His people forgot God in them, and they became formalities and traditions devoid of meaning. The people were far from God; religious, yet not spiritual. We must guard against the same error. Yet, a body was prepared for the Lord to become that one glorious offering by which we have been sanctified. He came to do the will of God, delighting in it; and He did it wholly and acceptably, God delighting in Him. "For by one offering He has perfected for all time those who are sanctified" (Hebrews 10:14).

Though He is chosen of God, the kings and rulers of the earth take their stand "against the LORD and against His Anointed" (Psalm 2:2), but "He who Sits in the heavens laughs, the Lord scoffs at them" (v.4). The time is coming very soon when the Lord will take His rightful place on the throne of earth in the millennium of peace, because He has already been installed upon Zion by His God. He is the One to whom God speaks in His absolute delight, "Thou art My Son, today I have begotten Thee" (Psalm 2:7; cf. Hebrews 1:5).

To no one else has He ever said that, not even to the angels who do what He bids without hesitation. But to the Lord Jesus Christ, His only begotten Son, He has given "the nations as Thine inheritance, and the very ends of the earth as Thy possession. Thou shalt break them with a rod of iron, Thou shalt shatter them like earthenware" (vv. 8-9). When He comes again to His own, He'll come in absolute majesty to reign, and there will be none who can stand against Him in that day to reject Him as King. He is King, He is Lord, and He is coming in all authority; the One rejected by men, but with God, "elect, precious".

Psalm 41:9 and Psalm 55:12-14 give us something of the anguish that David felt at being betrayed by a close friend, but also vividly portray the anguish of the Lord as Judas betrayed Him for thirty pieces of silver. The closeness of the friendship obviously escaped Judas, who did not appreciate the depth of the love of God in Christ, and he "lifted up his heel" against Him. "For it is not an enemy who reproaches Me, then I could bear it; nor is it one who hates Me who has exalted himself against Me, then I could hide Myself from him. But it is you, a man My equal, My companion and My familiar friend". "Friend, do what you have come for" (Matthew 26:50), said the Lord in the garden as Judas led the mob to take Him prisoner.

Oh, the depth of the love and grace of Christ! They had walked together for about three and a half years and "had sweet fellowship together ... in the house of God in the throng". Yet this was the one who delivered Him to the chief priests to be condemned and crucified. No wonder Peter referred to Psalm 69:25 and Psalm 109:8 when in Acts 1:20 he said about Judas, "Let his homestead be made desolate, and let no man dwell in it; and, His office let another man take".

What depth of anguish is seen in the words of Psalm 69. The Lord was the Man who walked, not in the counsel of the wicked, but in the counsel of God. He stood, not in the path of sinners, but in the path of God. Yet we find Him in a most fearful place. "I have sunk in deep mire, and there is no foothold; I have come into deep waters, and a flood overflows Me". This One who walked firmly in the path of God must sink in the deep mire as He bore in His body all our sin. He must be baptized with the flood of God's wrath for sin. How this distressed Him during His life until it was accomplished (Luke 12:50). No wonder that on the Cross His throat was parched (69:3), not with crying, for Christ opened not His mouth, but with the agony of what He was enduring at the hand of His God who had turned from Him. He quoted from this Psalm Himself in John 15:25 as He reflected on the hatred of men: "Those who hate Me without a cause are more than the hairs of My head".

Then we see in verse 4 something of the truth of the trespass offering, of which Christ was the Antitype and more: "What I did not steal, I then have to restore". Though Christ was sinless, He restored all that had been removed by sin, plus a whole lot more than the twenty per cent that the trespass offering required. "He made Him who knew no sin to be sin on our behalf, that we might become the righteousness of God in Him" (2 Corinthians 5:21). We've been taken from being dead in our transgressions, to being made alive together with Christ; and we've been raised with Him and seated in the heavenlies in Christ Jesus, "in order that in the ages to come He might show the surpassing riches of His grace in kindness toward us in Christ Jesus" Ephesians 2:5-7). What a restoration of that which He did not steal!

Psalm 69:8 shows the rejection that the Lord experienced at the hands of His own household (see John 7:3-5). Verse 9 explains, however, that the household with which He was most concerned was that of His God and Father. He was never rejected there! "For zeal for Thy house has consumed Me". It was not zeal for dead tradition and inactive formality, but zeal for a house where God was living and active. The house had value only because there was a living God associated with it, whom the Lord loved with all His heart and soul and mind. The value of the house has not changed. And yet, the One who so delighted the God of the house was heart-broken by reproach "I am so sick. And I looked for sympathy, but there was none, and for comforters, but I found none. They also gave Me gall for My food, and for My thirst they gave Me vinegar to drink".

The nation of Israel crucified the Lord of glory, their Messiah, their King, the One who thrilled the heart of God. They rejected Him outright, they horribly mistreated Him. But He was and is God's Chosen. "Therefore, let all the house of Israel know for certain that God has made Him both Lord and Christ - this Jesus whom you crucified" (Acts 2:36). He's on the throne of God and one day soon Psalm 69:34-36 will come to pass. He'll be rejected no more! He'll be the center of God's kingdom, on a throne that is rightfully His. And we'll praise Him forever, God's chosen One in whom His soul delights (Isaiah 42:1).

All Scripture quotations are from the NASB.

CHAPTER TEN: THE ANGUISH OF THE CRUCIFIED (JOHN ARCHIBALD)

―――

These two Psalms are ascribed to David and this is confirmed in the case of Psalm 69 by Romans 11:9. They contain unmistakable references to the sufferings of Christ on the Cross, and direct quotations from both Psalms are found in the New Testament Gospel narratives.

David, a man after God's heart, has been used by the Holy Spirit to give us a glimpse of the events of Calvary as they were experienced by the Occupant of the central Cross. As we read and consider these intimate and deeply moving portions of the Word, our hearts are challenged through another prophet, "Is it nothing to you, all ye that pass by? Behold, and see if there be any sorrow like unto My sorrow, which is done unto Me" (Lamentations 1:12).

BODILY ANGUISH (Psalm 22:14-16; 69:3,21)

Among the many amazing implications of the manhood of Christ was His direct experience of physical distress in His body. The thoughtful believer is filled with wonder on reading of One who is Mighty God, sitting by the well near Sychar, wearied with His journey. Acknowledging the all-sufficiency of God, David wrote "The eyes of all wait upon Thee; and Thou givest them their meat in due season". Yet we read of God the Son being hungry after forty days in the wilderness of Judea. How great then is the marvel of Golgotha, where the King eternal, the only God, endured the bodily suffering that is so graphically portrayed in these Psalms.

First we consider the physical weariness and weakness expressed in the words "I am poured out like water" and "My heart is like wax; it is melted in the midst of My bowels" and "My strength is dried up like a potsherd". At Calvary He reached the end of His earthly journey, in which so much had been accomplished, "I must go on My way today and tomorrow and the day following: for it cannot be that a prophet perish out of Jerusalem" (Luke 13:33). Unlike the journey that took Him to Sychar, there was no rest for Him when He reached His lifelong destination at the place of sacrifice. He suffered all the stress of those last days and hours before His arrest, and then the violence of the soldiers, the buffeting, the flogging and the thorns on His brow; followed by the burden of the Cross on His bleeding back as He set out for the appointed place. Surely the One who "by His strength setteth fast the mountains," was crucified through weakness (Psalm 65:6; 2 Corinthians 13:4).

Weariness was accompanied by pain that was widespread, "all My bones are out of joint", and sharply focussed, "they pierced My hands and My feet". The apostle John received the future promise, "Behold ... death shall be no more ... nor pain, any more" (Revelation 21:3-4). Is it not wonderful that the Supreme Ruler sitting on the throne from which the abolition of pain is proclaimed, has Himself known the unremitting pangs of bodily pain as He hung in weakness on the tree of shame? And there was no voice from the throne proclaiming relief for Him on that dark day.

Along with the weakness and the pain came thirst. "My tongue cleaveth to My jaws" and "My throat is dried" and "In My thirst they gave Me vinegar to drink". From the account in John chapter 19 we learn that at the last He said, "I thirst". This is the only recorded instance of an audible comment from Him on the Cross about His physical distress. He gave one last opportunity for mankind to show Him kindness, and they responded with vinegar. With the bitterness from that final act of hostility searing His parched mouth and lips He said "It is finished".

ANGUISH OF MIND AND HEART (Psalm 22:6-8, 17-18 & 69:4,8-9,19-20)

At the same time as the body of the Lord Jesus was racked with pain there were deeper sorrows of the heart and mind to augment His anguish and we are given some insight into these.

Consider the shame and humiliation described: "they look and stare upon Me: they part My garments among them, and upon My vesture do they cast lots", and "shame hath covered My face". The Roman soldiers spat upon His face. For them to spit in the face of Tiberius Caesar would have brought instant death and the very idea would have filled them with terror, but they spat in the face of the King of kings. They took His clothes and gambled for the coat without seam, while onlookers and passers-by stared at the unclad Sufferer. In heaven the mighty seraphim habitually covered their faces and their feet in His presence; on earth the congregation of evil doers stripped Him' and stared.

There was also scorn. "A reproach of men, and despised of the people. All they that see Me laugh Me to scorn". The mighty

Saviour was openly despised by the wretched creatures who were totally dependent upon Him for life and breath and all things. He knew their hearts, they did not need to speak for Him to understand their thoughts, so that those who despised Him in silence were also known to Him. Of the many bitter taunts that were hurled at the Christ that day, perhaps the one that caused Him most grief was the use of Psalm 22 by the chief priests, scribes and elders of Israel when they said, "He trusteth on God; let Him deliver Him now, if He desireth Him" (Matthew 27:43). It was and always will be true that God delights in His blessed Son. The men who uttered the challenge were leaders of the people that God had acknowledged as His own. Truly, "they that were His own received Him not". We cannot appreciate how acute was the suffering caused by this emphasis of God's purpose not to spare His only begotten Son.

He died broken-hearted. The causeless hatred of men and their rejection of Him constituted a crushing burden of reproach that broke His heart. "They that hate Me without a cause are more than the hairs of Mine head". The history of mankind is a history of rejection of God. It began with Adam's choice to disregard the command of God. The rejection acquired a new dimension at Babel when that first kingdom of men established its aims and purpose without reference to the Lord. He was given no place in their affairs.

Later, when God established a kingdom of His own, the nation of Israel whom He had chosen repeatedly failed to honour Him, and rejected His pleading and His messengers. Finally God sent His son, and men rejected Him. Even those who had been so highly favoured as the people of God would not receive the Son. For the Messiah this was a deep and piercing sorrow. "I am become a stranger unto My brethren, and an alien unto My mother's children. For the zeal of Thine house hath eaten Me up". Desire for the house and kingdom of God was a consuming passion with the Son, but those who should have been the builders rejected the Corner Stone (Mat. 21:42-43). He died without pity or comfort In His incomparable anguish He was entirely alone.

THE ANGUISH OF DEITY (Psalm 22:1; 69:1-2, 1-15, 26)

In our review, of the anguish of the Crucified we come now to depths of horror that we shall never plumb. We believe that the deepest anguish of Calvary concerned the bearing of sin, the experience of death and what God did to His only Son. "Him who knew no sin He made to be sin on our behalf" (2 Corinthians 5:21). The abhorrence of sin by Deity was invoked to the ultimate in the experience of the Saviour at Calvary. The anguish to Him of bearing our sins in His body on the tree lies far beyond our comprehension.

His anguish at the experience of death is indicated in the appeal, "Let not the pit shut her mouth upon Me". The Prince of Life, who gave and sustains the life of all flesh, was to die Himself. There was no other way. The Anointed One must be cut off. He became obedient "even unto death, yea, the death of the Cross". David was able to say, "Yea, though I walk through the valley of the shadow of death, I will fear no evil; for Thou art with me", but David's Lord traversed that dark valley alone, without protector or companion.

Lastly, we contemplate the deep mystery of God's dealings with His Son on the Cross. We hear the cry of chilling intensity from

Deity to Deity, "My God, My God, why hast Thou forsaken Me?" It tells of desolation beyond measure. The One who cried is the One of whom it is written "In the beginning was the Word, and the Word was with God, and the Word was God" (John 1:1). On the night before Calvary He spoke to God His Father about "the glory which I had with Thee before the world was" (John 17:5). Calvary is the only point in eternity where this forsaking takes place. But more even than this is found in Psalm 69, following the passage which speaks of the lack of comforters and the activities of His persecutors. "For they persecute Him whom Thou hast smitten". The prophecy of Zechariah also speaks of this awaking of the sword of divine judgement to find its deadly mark in the One who is all God's pleasure. Again, we struggle to comprehend the mystery of Deity punishing Deity, and what it must have meant for the blessed One who was so smitten.

In all the accumulated anguish we have considered, we hear the language of His soul, "I sink in deep mire, where there is no standing: I am come into deep waters, where the floods overflow Me", and "deliver Me out of the mire, and let Me not sink". The One who upholds all things by the Word of His power finds no protection and has nowhere to stand. "Deep calleth unto deep at the noise of Thy cataracts: all Thy waves and Thy billows are gone over Me" (Psalm 42:7 RVM). For ever blessed be His name.

CHAPTER ELEVEN: CHRIST RAISED AND GLORIFIED (JIM SEDDON)

———

"**B**ut now hath Christ been raised from the dead" (1 Corinthians 15:20). These were the emphatic words of Paul to the Corinthians - words born out of reality. At the time they were written, the resurrected Lord Jesus had occupied the throne of heaven for almost thirty years. A statement such as Paul's testifies to the immutability of God's Word concerning His Son's resurrection and glory. The Old Testament is a mine full of promises pertaining to Christ, and one of the richest veins in which the promises are found is the Psalms. For example: "Thou wilt not leave My soul to Sheol; neither wilt Thou suffer Thine Holy One to see corruption" (16:10). Paul quotes these words of David in Acts 13:35, thus forming signposts in the New Testament as well as the Old, that ever point upward as did the two heavenly messengers who appeared to the women at the garden tomb and said: "He is not here, but is risen" (Luke 24:6).

This note of victory, that first sounded in the ears of the Lord's disciples on earth, reached its crescendo in heaven where the innumerable host of angelic beings honoured and worshipped the ascended Lord: Lift up your heads, O ye gates; and be ye lift up, ye everlasting doors: and the King of glory shall come in. Who is the King of glory? The LORD strong and mighty, the LORD mighty in battle ... The LORD of hosts, He is the King of glory (Psalm 24:7-8,10). The Lord of hosts passed through the heavens, entering triumphantly as the King of glory. The longing of His heart had now been realized: "Glorify Thou Me with Thine own self with the glory which I had with Thee before the world was" (John 17:5). Isaiah's Man of sorrows had become the Psalmist's Man of praise: "Thy salvation, O God, set Me up on high. I will praise the Name of God with a song, and will magnify Him with thanksgiving" (Psalm 69:29-30).

Such praise and adoration is reciprocal within the Godhead as the Father takes up the refrain to His Son: "Thy throne, O God, is for ever and ever: a sceptre of equity is the sceptre of Thy kingdom. Thou hast loved righteousness, and hated wickedness: therefore God, Thy God, hath anointed Thee with the oil of gladness above Thy fellows (Psalm 45:6-7). We too, with John, can rejoice as we hear afresh: "His voice as the voice of many waters ... saying, Fear not; I am the first and the last, and the Living One; 'and I was dead, and behold, I am alive for evermore (Revelation 1:15,17,18).

"God highly exalted Him" (Philippians 2:9)

There were certain Greeks that came to Philip saying, "Sir, we would see Jesus" (John 12:21), and when the Lord was told He said, "The hour is come, that the Son of Man should be glorified" (v.23). Those Greeks together with the Jews were representative of the whole of the human race amongst whom Christ must be glorified. The word in the Greek New Testament translated glorified means "to magnify, extol, praise, especially of glorifying God, i.e., ascribing honour to Him" (Vine). His very Being demands no less than this.

Each Person of the Godhead commands equal honour (John 5:22,23). In despising and rejecting the Son, men failed to glorify God. Nevertheless, God must be glorified through His Son: "Father, glorify Thy Name. There came therefore a voice out of heaven, saying, I have both glorified it, and will glorify it again" (John 12:28). In the events leading up to the crucifixion the voice of rebellion sounded loud and clear. In response to Pilate's exclamation, "Behold your King!" they replied, "Away with Him, crucify Him ... we have no king but Caesar" (John 19:14-15). But in His resurrection power and glory the Son is addressed by the Father: "Sit Thou at My right hand, until I make Thine enemies Thy footstool" (Psalm 110:1).

If men do not give Christ His rightful place, then God will. When Pilate asked the multitude, "What then shall I do unto Jesus which is called Christ? They all say, Let Him be crucified" (Matthew 27:22). A very different picture is presented in the words of King Ahasuerus to the wicked Haman concerning Mordecai, which illustrate the purpose of God in relation to the Lord Jesus: "What shall be done unto the man whom the king delighteth to honour?" (Esther 6:6). Haman mistakenly assumed he was about to be honoured and replied, in effect "Glorify him, treat him like royalty". The result was that the despised Mordecai was exalted and treated like a prince.

The love and esteem of the Father for the Son is an expression of the perfect reciprocal relationship within the Godhead. But unregenerate men and women display a hostile attitude to the Father and the Son: "the mind of the flesh is enmity against God" (Romans 8:7). Nevertheless, the Son demands and will receive the honour that is due to Him. The Father has highly exalted the Son and given Him "the Name which is above every name; that in the Name of Jesus every knee should bow and that every tongue should confess that Jesus Christ is Lord, to the glory of God the Father" (Philippians 2:9-11).

Speaking through His servant Isaiah, God said, "I am the LORD (Jehovah, the Self-existent One); that is My Name: and My glory will I not give to another" (Isaiah 42:8). Yet, in a future day under the influence of the false prophet, many will seek to take away glory from God by blasphemously rendering divine honours to antichrist, the man of sin. In the second Psalm God leaves us in no doubt as to whom glory belongs and with whom it will ever remain. The Father says of the exaltation of His Son:

> "I have set My King upon My holy hill of Zion. I will tell of the decree: the LORD said unto Me, Thou art My Son; this day have I begotten Thee. Ask of Me, and I will give Thee the nations for Thine inheritance, and the uttermost parts of the earth for Thy possession. Thou shalt break them with a rod of iron; Thou shalt dash them in pieces like a potter's vessel" (2:6-9).

During the glorious millennial reign of the Lord Jesus Christ, the words of Solomon will be on the lips of many: "Blessed be the LORD God, the God of Israel, who only doeth wondrous things: and blessed be His glorious Name for ever; and let the whole earth be filled with His glory. Amen, and Amen" (Psalm 72:18-19). It was in His raised and glorified body that the Lord ascended to heaven. The Victor of Calvary, the King of glory, is appointed by the Father "a Priest for ever after the order of Melchizedek" (Psalm 110:4). It is still true of our Lord Jesus Christ as it was of old that

His "delight" is "with the sons of men" (Proverbs 8:31). Upon the Cross as Substitute, He suffered the judgement of God for our sins. As Son and Great High Priest over the house of God, He represents God's people in the heavenly sanctuary. Apart from the day of atonement, Aaron, the high priest of Israel, wore garments that were for "glory and for beauty" foreshadowing the glories and beauties of Christ. Upon the onyx stones that rested on the shoulders of Aaron and also upon the precious stones in his breastplate were engraved the names of the twelve tribes of Israel as he represented the nation before God (Exodus 28:6-30).

The typical significance of this in relation to the Lord Jesus Christ is well expressed by the hymn writer:

On His heart our names are graven,

On His shoulders we are borne.

For His sake the Father loves us;

Praise becomes us in return.

The writer to the Hebrews says, "Both He that sanctifieth (the Son) and they that are sanctified are all of One (the Father): for which cause He is not ashamed to call them brethren" (Hebrews 2:11). In expressing the relationship into which He has brought God's new covenant people the Lord says, "I will declare Thy Name unto My brethren: in the midst of the congregation will I praise Thee" (Psalm 22:22). Through the Psalmist God said (and it applies under both covenants): "Gather My saints together unto Me; those that have made a covenant with Me by sacrifice" (50:5). When God's people are together as a Holy Priesthood, the ascended Lord presents their praise to the God and Father of our Lord Jesus Christ.

We may sum up by saying of the faithful Man of Psalm 22, that He is also the blessed Man of Psalm 1; He was the suffering Man of Psalm 22; who became the exalted Man of Psalm 24; and He will be the reigning Man of Psalm 2. But what shall we say of the present? Although the Victor of Calvary is, for the most part, "despised and rejected of men"; although many still "esteem Him not", it is our privilege to rejoice with David and say "I will bless the LORD at all times: His praise shall continually be in my mouth ... O magnify the LORD with me, and let us exalt His Name together" (Psalm 34:1,3). May it be so until He comes, for His Name's sake.

CHAPTER TWELVE: WORLD PEACE AT LAST (ALEX REID)

———

Since the dawn of human history when the first man born of woman rose up and slew his brother (Genesis 4:1-15), the record of human civilization is one of the continual clash of rival aspirations; of individuals, races, nations and political ideologies. The ebb and flow of such conflicts leaves behind a host of innocent victims. The God of heaven is not ignorant of or indifferent to this situation. The time is fast drawing near when God will intervene directly in human affairs, put right all injustices and usher in a golden age of world peace.

One would image that such an idea would be whole-heartedly embraced by mankind; alas the contrary is true. The nations of the world today, in general, reject any thought of restraint or order being imposed upon them by God. What is true of the nations today was true also of the nations in David's day, as he wrote in the second Psalm (vv. 1-3). But such an opposition is foolish and futile in the extreme, for the purposes of God are fixed and determined, His purpose being that His chosen King will reign from Zion (Psalm 2:4-6). In David the psalmist's day, he was the chosen king, but through David's words the Holy Spirit was looking forward to One greater than David who was yet to come (see Luke 1:32-33).

Psalm 2 was written as a royal decree, verses 7-9 being the heart of its declaration. This is God's decree concerning His beloved Son who will rule in power throughout the world (Psalm

2:8,9.47:2,3.72:8,11); this decree having gone forth, it will never be rescinded. Those nations who think they can oppose God's will with their own plans and purposes, are on a collision course with God's appointed King, and before the golden age of peace can be brought in it is necessary that there be a ...

Prelude to Peace

Given that the nations and their rulers have set themselves against the Lord and His anointed (Psalm 2:2), it is necessary that the power and pride of the nations be broken and they become subservient to Christ before the era of peace can begin. These momentous events are foreseen in the Psalms, for example Psalms 2, 45 and 110.

The nations and their leaders in their self-will and opposition are described as the King's enemies (Psalm 45:5; 110:1-2), but they are enemies who will not prosper and whose power will be broken out of hand (Psalm 2:9; 45:5). The King in Psalm 45 is exhorted to gird on His sword and enter into contention with the rebels, the result of which will be their utter defeat (Psalm 45:3-4). These are the days of battle when Christ will subdue those who have gathered to destroy Israel and oppose Messiah's rule (Psalm 46:6; 110:5,6. Cf. Isaiah 63:1-6; Revelation 16:12-16; 19:11-16).

The Aftermath of Armageddon

As a result of their defeat at the last great battle of the age, there will be a reversal of attitude among the nations of the world. Instead of opposition and hatred, the kings and great ones of the earth will bow before the exalted Christ, kissing His feet and presenting their gifts (Psalm 2:12,22:27-28 & 72:9-11). Their demeanour will then be that of reverent worshippers blessing His name and calling Him happy (Psalm 47:1,8,9; 72:17). In their subjection to Christ, the nations will discover a joy and fulfilment not experienced before (Psalm 2:11,12), as at last they learn to be still in their spirits and renounce their former turbulent natures (Psalm 46:10 see also Revised Version Margin). The most welcome corollary of this new-found spirit among the nations will be world-wide cessation from war and armed conflict and the doing away with weapons of war and mass destruction (Psalm 46:9 cf. Isaiah 2:4; Micah 4:3).

The Changed Environment of Earth

As well as this change of heart among the nations there will be physical changes throughout the earth at the onset of the reign of peace. Upheavals of great magnitude seem to be anticipated (Psalm 46:1-3), perhaps connected with the coming of the Son of Man and the manifestation of His judgement upon the nations at that time (see also Revelation 6:14; 16:20). The environs of Jerusalem and the land of Israel will be changed, as the city which today has no river flowing through it will be nurtured by one issuing forth from the House of God in those days (Psalm 46:4 cf. Isaiah 33:21; Ezekiel 47:1-12).

The earth once cursed because of the entrance of sin into the world and duly grudgingly giving of her fruits (Genesis 3:17-19) will then yield bountiful harvests, so that want and starvation will not be known among the nations (Psalm 72:16).

Jerusalem and Israel

We have noted the change of attitude to Christ that will be displayed by the nations in a coming day, but no less remarkable and perhaps more so, will be the changed attitude of the Jewish people to the once despised Jesus of Nazareth. The people that once denied His claim to Kingship and rejected His rule (John 19:15), will then have looked on Him whom they pierced (John 19:37; Revelation 1:7) and praise and glorify Him, standing in awe of His person (Psalm 22:23). Repentant Israel will be given a place at the head of the nations and receive their inheritance from the Lord (Psalm 47:3-4). Zion, the city of Jerusalem, will become the dwelling place of Messiah (Psalm 46:4-5) and the administrative centre from which His rule will go forth (Psalm 110:2). As the favoured people of the Lord the Jew will be held in high esteem among the peoples of the nations (Zechariah 8:22-23).

The Administration of Peace

An administration or government takes its character from the one who is its bead, so the character of Christ's reign of peace will be derived from the character of the Lord Himself. The Psalms leave us with a very clear picture of the glories and virtues of Christ that will be displayed to all in the coming kingdom.

Psalm 45:2 witnesses to the words of grace that the subject nations will bear from the lips of the living, Messiah. Just as those who in a former day in Nazareth, "wondered at the words of grace which proceeded out of His mouth" (Luke 4:22), so the peoples will wonder as the Prince of Peace speaks peace to the nations (Zechariah 9:10). The personal prestige of the King derive from His traits of meekness and righteousness (Psalm 45:4,7); and His love of what is true and right will manifest itself in the equity and justice that will be the hallmarks of His reign (Psalm 45:6; 72:2). Using a figure of speech to illustrate the effect of this marvellous and beneficial rule, the psalmist says: "He shall come down like rain upon the mown grass: as showers that water the earth. In His days shall the righteous flourish; and abundance of peace till the moon be no more" (Psalm 72:6-7).

The Effect of Peace

God says of the Lord Jesus in Psalm 110 verse 4: "Thou art a Priest for ever after the order of Melchizedek". The writer to the Hebrews, commenting on Melchizedek says: "For this Melchizedek, king of Salem, priest of God Most High, who met Abraham returning from the slaughter of the kings, and blessed him ... being first, by interpretation, king of righteousness, and then also king of Salem, which is, king of peace" (Hebrews 7:1-2).

The person of Melchizedek combines the offices of king and priest, and his ministry was one of sustaining and refreshing to the pilgrim Abraham (see Genesis 14:17-20). In the coming kingdom of peace, the Lord Jesus, Priest after the order of Melchizedek, King of righteousness and King of peace, will pour forth His ministry of blessing and refreshing on the oppressed and needy.

The poor, meek, oppressed and needy of the earth will rejoice in the days of the King-Priest's reign, for the cries of the needy and afflicted will be heard and the meek satisfied (Psalm 22:24,26), the poor and oppressed will receive justice, pity, salvation, and deliverance from oppression both physical and financial (Psalm 72:4, 12:14). These are the times when the poor in spirit, the meek and persecuted will indeed be blessed, for they shall inherit the earth and theirs will be the kingdom of heaven (Matthew 5:3,5,10). When the Lord Jesus sits as king and priest upon His throne then, truly the work and effect of righteousness will he experienced; peace, quietness and confidence for ever (Zechariah 6:13 & Isaiah 33:17).

CHAPTER THIRTEEN: ZION, THE CITY OF GOD (JOHN DRAIN)

It is very evident in the Scriptures that God has revealed Himself and has worked from several centres. An analysis of the revelation relating to this line of truth will confirm that no place has had greater prominence than Zion. Zion as a centre of divine and human activity can be seen in the past, in the present and in the future.

Looking towards the future we can anticipate the time when, the fulness of the Gentiles having come in, God will grant repentance and restoration to Israel. This will be the glorious day of receiving back His people whom He put away in righteous anger. When the King of Israel, our Lord Jesus Christ, establishes His millennial reign, His centre will be Jerusalem. The words of Joel 3:17 will then have fulfilment, "So shall ye know that I am the LORD your God, dwelling in Zion My holy mountain: then shall Jerusalem be holy, and there shall no strangers pass through her any more." In that day this divine centre will be acknowledged by all. "And the sons of them that afflicted thee shall come bending unto thee; and all they that despised thee shall bow themselves down at the soles of thy feet; and they shall call thee The city of the LORD, The Zion of the Holy One of Israel" (Isaiah 60:14).

In this present dispensation God's dwelling place on earth is a spiritual house. Its existence and manifestation are related to the fact which Peter quotes when, referring to the purpose of God realized in believers in Christ being built up a spiritual house, he says, "Because it is contained in scripture, Behold, I lay in Zion a chief corner Stone, elect, precious" (1 Peter 2:6). This Stone is the Son of God, the Lord Jesus Christ. Hence in Hebrews 12, when contrasting the experience of the Israel people of old with that of God's people in this present dispensation, the writer says, "But ye are come unto Mount Zion, and unto the city of the living God, the heavenly Jerusalem ..." (Hebrews 12:22). In the heavenly realm there is this great divine centre of activity and the importance and implications of its existence should be carefully considered by all who are exercised to do the will of God.

In this chapter we wish more particularly to draw attention to the Zion of a past day, and to examine some scriptures which help us to appreciate something of the purpose of God which was associated with that earthly centre. In so doing we have before us that there are basic principles of divine purpose which abide through all ages, and we can learn from the past for the present.

Psalm 78 is an impressive record of the LORD's dealings with His people, and it was given so that succeeding generations might be acquainted with what God had done. In verses 67-69 we reach a very serious crisis in God's workings when we read, "Moreover He refused the tent of Joseph, and chose not the tribe of Ephraim; but chose the tribe of Judah, the mount Zion which He loved. And He built His sanctuary like the heights ..." The place which divine election has in divine purposes is worthy of close examination. God has made choice of peoples and persons and places, and He is not answerable to anyone as to the choice He makes. The wickedness of God's people had compelled Him to turn away from His place in Shiloh. But the time came when the LORD revealed that the place of His choice was Zion in the inheritance of Judah. We read, "For the LORD hath chosen Zion; He hath desired it for His habitation. This is My resting place for ever: here will I dwell; for I have desired it" (Psalm 132:13-14). God's choice of Zion was final. Though He had recurring sorrow from the disobedience of His people, the LORD never chose another earthly centre.

Zion was not only the place of God's desire and choice; it was the place upon which His affection rested. In one of the songs of the sons of Korah it is stated, "The LORD loveth the gates of Zion more than all the dwellings of Jacob. Glorious things are spoken of thee, O city of God" (Psalm 87:2,8). God had a very deep love for Zion. It was the place on earth He chose in which to dwell, and one of the glorious things which could be spoken about Zion was that God, the eternal One of infinite attributes, dwelt there. The writer of Psalm 74 pleads with God, "Remember Thy congregation ... and mount Zion, wherein Thou hast dwelt."

Zion was a place worthy of the God who chose it. In Psalm 48 we have the lovely words, "Great is the LORD, and highly to be praised, in the city of our God, in His holy mountain. Beautiful in elevation, the joy of the whole earth, is mount Zion, on the sides of the north, the city of the great King" (Psalm 48:1-2). Her towers, her bulwarks, her palaces were well worthy of reverent and careful consideration.

This remarkable centre was not only the place where God dwelt. It was also the great centre from which God was revealed. "Out of Zion, the perfection of beauty, God hath shined forth" (Psalm 50:2). "The LORD hath built up Zion, He hath appeared in His glory" (Psalm 102:16). God reveals Himself to draw men and women to Himself. And so we are led to the conclusion that God's centre in Zion became the great centre of affection and interest for those who loved the LORD and who longed after Him.

When David took Jerusalem and the stronghold of Zion from the Jebusites, it is clear that he was working in the way of divine desire and purpose. He was securing the site which was to mean so much to God. The fulfilment of God's purposes can extend to men the privilege of working for God, and happy are they who are found so engaged.

The revelation of God in Zion led exercised hearts to know God in wondrous measure. In Psalm 2 we read, "Yet I have set My King upon My holy hill of Zion". Whatever may be the full scope of these words, we can at least see that associated with Zion is the kingly authority of the LORD. The majestic words of Psalm 99 tell us, "The LORD reigneth; let the peoples tremble; He sitteth upon the cherubim; let the earth be moved. The LORD is great in Zion; and He is high above all the peoples. Let them praise Thy great and terrible name Holy is He."

This aspect of the revelation of God is of great importance because it emphasizes that the authority of God is manifested in Zion. "Out of Zion shall go forth the law, and the word of the LORD from Jerusalem" (Isaiah 2:3). The King rules by His law, and His word embodies His authority. It was the purpose of God that from His centre Zion His law and His word would be transmitted to reach the homes and the hearts of all Israel.

When David brought up the ark of God and put it in the tent which he had pitched for it in the city of David, he introduced a new feature into the service of the people of Israel in relation to worship. This he did by the commandment of the LORD. We read, "Then on that day did David first ordain to give thanks unto the LORD, by the hand of Asaph and his brethren" (1 Chronicles 16:7). As a result, "All the people said, Amen, and praised the LORD" (1 Chronicles 16:36). In Psalm 65 David wrote, "Praise waiteth for Thee, O God, in Zion and unto Thee shall the vow be performed. O Thou that hearest prayer, unto Thee shall all flesh come."

Zion resounded with the praise of God. The songs of Zion released the emotions pent in the hearts of those who appreciated what the LORD had done for them. David exhorted, "Sing praises to the Lord, which dwelleth in Zion: Declare among the people His doings" (Psalm 9:11).

He not only exhorted others to do so. He himself pleaded with the Lord to have mercy upon him and to deliver him so "That I may shew forth all Thy praise in the gates of the daughter of Zion, I will rejoice in Thy salvation" (Psalm 9:14). When the people of Judah found themselves in Babylon they wept when they remembered Zion. Zion and its songs of praise meant much to the godly Israelite, and when these songs could no longer be sung, sorrowful weeping took the place of joyful singing. When their captors requested to hear one of the songs of Zion back came the sad response from the children of Israel, "How shall we sing the LORD's song in a strange land?" (Psalm 137:4). Zion's songs were for the God who dwelt in Zion.

Psalm 65 shows not only that praise is associated with Zion, but also that in this great centre there is the activity of prayer. There dwelt the God who heard prayer and who delighted to answer those who put their trust in Him. From Zion emanated the blessing of God. The words of Psalm 128:4-5 supply a thought here. "Behold, that thus shall the man be blessed that feareth the LORD. The LORD shall bless thee out of Zion ... "The blessing of God is manifold and variegated, and is related to many aspects of human need. As we think of Zion we are reminded of the words of Isaiah 14:32, "The LORD hath founded Zion, and in her shall the afflicted of His people take refuge." David had some such thought in mind when he said, "The LORD answer thee in the day of trouble. The name of the God of Jacob set thee up on high. Send thee help from the sanctuary, and strengthen thee out of Zion" (Psalm 20:1-2).

Thus we see that as men learned concerning the purpose of God in Zion they appreciated something of this great centre as the place of His residence and His rule, as the place of rejoicing and refuge. It is sad to reflect that such glorious possibilities as Zion presented did not hold the people of God. Jeremiah is caused to write, "The ways of Zion do mourn, because none come to the solemn assembly; all her gates are desolate, her priests do sigh. Her virgins are afflicted, and she herself is in bitterness. And from the daughter of Zion all her majesty is departed. Jerusalem hath grievously sinned; therefore she is become as an unclean thing" (Lamentations 1:4,6,8).

Sin is a dreadful thing in the sight of God. Great blessings and privileges have been forfeited because of sin. Let those who know the will of God beware!

CHAPTER FOURTEEN: THE FEELING OF BEING OVERWHELMED! (JACK FERGUSON)

───

M any a dear saint of God has been overwhelmed. It is a human experience, which knows no confines of time or space. At one time or another, in the lives of most, and even the most devoted, the heart is overwhelmed. It may be that you are, even at the present moment.

The word "overwhelmed" occurs only eight times in our English Bible and each instance is in the Book of Psalms. Somehow this is not surprising, for to which other book does the heart so naturally turn in trouble? Luther called it "A Bible in miniature". Many of these precious psalms were written in days of affliction, to be read, century after century, by others experiencing similar difficulties. Similar, though probably quite different. It was often the persecution of enemies which overwhelmed the psalmists and that is sadly shared by many of our brothers and sisters in the world today. But for most of us it is the affliction of our circumstances.

Three different Hebrew words are translated "overwhelmed" in the eight occurrences, as shown in the footnote. These Hebrew words are translated into other English words elsewhere in Scripture, but for the moment we are only thinking of "overwhelmed", and in particular of ATAPH only - shrouded as in darkness. This is so real a description of the overwhelmed heart. The word occurs in five psalms, as shown in the footnote.

David wrote three of these psalms, 61, 142 and 143, the second being written "in the cave". Asaph wrote one of them, 77. But an unknown writer gave us Psalm 102. And in that anonymity many a dear saint has seen himself or herself. It is "A prayer of the afflicted", in the darkness of his circumstances, the pouring out of his complaint before the God in whom he trusted. Maybe the word "complaint" here gives a slightly wrong impression. The Hebrew equivalent is also translated "meditation". It comes from a root meaning to ponder, and by implication to utter one's thoughts aloud.

All unknown to others, many of God's children are, at this present time, calling on the Lord out of an overwhelmed heart; not necessarily complaining in their affliction, but simply in their deep inward musings calling out, "Why?" And no one understands better than the Lord Jesus. For He Himself called one day out of the darkness which enshrouded Him, "Why...?" So He understands. Maybe some overwhelmed heart, reading these lines, would like to take time to go through the five psalms referred to, that is 61, 77, 102, 142 and 143. If you do, the Holy Spirit will give you His own ministry from them, peculiarly and directly from Him to you in your own circumstances.

It may be in Psalm 61 the thought of the great Rock (v.2), the refuge, the strong tower (v.3), the covert of His wings (v.4) will bring comfort.

It may be in Psalm 77 a consideration of earlier experiences (v.6), a remembrance of help in past days (v.11), a meditation on His works, a musing on His doings (v.12) will bring cheer.

It may be in Psalm 142 the fact that God knows your path (v.3), that He is your refuge and portion (v.5) will bring strength.

It may be in Psalm 143 as you remember, meditate and muse (v.5), your overwhelmed spirit will so respond, as David's did, that you will say aloud to the Lord,

> Cause me to hear Thy loving kindness (v.8),
>
> Cause me to know the way (v.8),
>
> Deliver me, O LORD (v.9),
>
> Teach me (v.10),
>
> Quicken me (v.11).

Take courage, overwhelmed heart. Fay Inchtawn put it choicely, doubtless having Genesis 45:27 in mind. "For o'er your bare, brown, hopeless hill, The wagons may be coming, nearer still." They used to say, in the days of the shadows, "Thou hast beset me behind (the past) and before (the future), and laid Thine hand upon me (the present)" (Psalm 139:5). So all was well, and in those long past days overwhelmed hearts trusted Him. They came through fire and water is the strength of such promises as Isaiah 43:1-2: "But now thus saith the LORD that created thee ... formed thee ... redeemed thee ... called thee by thy name, thou art Mine. When thou passest through the waters, I will be with thee; and through the rivers, they shall not overflow thee: when thou walkest through the fire, thou shalt not be burned; neither shall the flame kindle upon thee".

But now the true light is shining, whereby we can say with even greater confidence, "And we know that to them that love God all things work together for good, even to them that are ... foreordained ... called ...justified ... glorified" (Romans 8:28-30). No wonder F.R. Havergal, musing in life's latest hours on Jude verse 1, commented, "Called ... beloved ... kept ... well I'll just go Home on that".

"Before us is a future all unknown,

A path untrod.

Behind us is a Friend, well loved,

That Friend is God."

Footnote:

KACAH, meaning to fill up or to cover. It occurs in Psalm 55:5 and 78:53. SHATAPH, meaning to gush or to inundate. It occurs in Psalm 124:4. ATAPH, meaning to shroud, as in darkness. It occurs in Psalm 61:2; 77:3; 102 (title); 142:3; 143:4 (All meanings from Dr Strong).

CHAPTER FIFTEEN: COMFORT FOR THE TRIED AND SORROWFUL (P. WATKINSON)

———

I t's good for us to cast our minds back in review over our lives, and recount how the Lord has made His presence known to us in one way or another in times of trouble; to view again those times of stress and difficulty when all seemed opposed to us, and we were in "deep waters"; when vain was the help of man, and we were cast upon our God, and when we knew the unfolding of God's plan for us and divine deliverance. Didn't our hearts rise in praise and thankfulness to God when deliverance came? Wasn't there a song in our heart as we saw again the evidence of God's care for us? Many of the psalms were the outcome of times of trouble, and they record the deliverance God wrought for the psalmists. Let us consider some written by David.

In Psalm 54:7 David writes, "He hath delivered me out of all trouble." According to the superscription to this psalm (RV), it was written when David was betrayed by the Ziphites (see 1 Samuel 23:19). David had fled from Saul who sought his life, and David was hiding in strongholds in the wood. News of the plot reached David, and it's in this setting that he writes this psalm of prayer for salvation. Note the sense of confidence, culminating in the words of verse 7 "He hath delivered me." The word "delivered" means "rescued." Just at the critical time when the opposing forces were approaching each other, Saul receives word that the land is invaded, and he has to return immediately. David's faith is rewarded and he is able to rejoice in his deliverance.

Psalm 63:7 (KJV): "Because Thou hast been my help, therefore in the shadow of Thy wings will I rejoice." This psalm was written while David was in the wilderness of Judah. He was being hunted from place to place. Yet, in circumstances calculated to cause anyone to be despondent and downcast, David is able to rejoice, for he has a Helper. Throughout his wilderness experience he knew the help of God, and his words indicate his trust in God. Knowing such a One assisting him he is able to rejoice, and rest in quiet confidence under the shadow of God's protecting wings, aware that nothing would befall him which would be to his disadvantage. David had mighty men of valour who would hazard their lives for him, but here was One above all others, who helped this humble man in all his difficulties. What a Helper is our God!

Psalm 3:5: "I laid me down and slept; I awaked; for the LORD sustained me." There are many experiences which men of God have been called upon to pass through, but perhaps the most testing was that of David when Absalom, his son, by wicked subtlety, turned the heart of the people away from David, and usurped his throne (2 Samuel 15:18). David was compelled to flee from Jerusalem, conscious that Absalom's desire was to slay him. Such is the background to Psalm 3. There were many who said of David at this time, "There is no help for him in God," but their words didn't discourage him. His faith was steadfast, and he experienced the support of the everlasting arms. In this assurance, he rests confidently, knowing that God, in His own way and time, would deliver him. He wasn't disturbed, for he knew that God was supplying all his need, and would never forsake him. Though tens of thousands set themselves against him, he had no fear. His faith was rewarded and in due time he was restored to his throne. Absalom met his untimely end hanging from a tree.

Psalm 18:18: Seated securely upon the throne, David reflects on his life and here pens something of his experiences. He remembers his calamities and the hatred he had known from his enemies. Yet he can testify, "But the LORD was my stay." He'd known in a very practical way the presence of God with him, staying him in moments of deep peril, when, left to his own resources, he would have failed and fallen. Close by his side was the LORD, strengthening him to meet the onslaughts of the enemy, and imparting courage to stand, and withstand. What an Eben-ezer to be able to raise, "but the LORD was my stay"! Never did he lack God's support in the trying circumstances of his life, and his psalms were written as the outcome of his experience with God. He knew God as his Deliverer, Helper, Sustainer and Supporter. Surely we, in our day, can have somewhat similar experiences to David

The Lord can be our Deliverer and take us out of all our troubles as He did David. The apostle Paul wrote of his own experience "God ... who delivered us out of so great a death, and will deliver ... on whom we have set our hope that He will also still deliver us" (2 Corinthians 1:10)

Do you feel imprisoned by adverse circumstances? Then look to the Lord, for He will deliver you out of them all if you trust in Him. He is ever ready to help us, and the writer of the epistle to the Hebrews records, "So that with good courage we say 'The Lord is my Helper I will not fear" (Hebrews 13:6). Nothing is too hard for the Lord, and if we confide in Him, we'll have the assurance of His assistance just when we need Him. Does the Lord sustain His people today? Of course He does! The words of Peter to elders can well be laid hold of by all God's children, "casting all your anxiety upon Him, because He careth for you" (1 Peter 5:7). This should calm our troubled hearts and induce calmness and assurance when we're in times of trouble. The apostle Paul testifies to the One who was his stay, "But the Lord stood by me, and strengthened me" (2 Timothy 4.17). God is the living God, the Deliverer, Helper, Sustainer and Supporter, if we will only trust in Him.

"Oh what peace we often forfeit,

Oh what needless pain we bear;

All because we do not carry

Everything to God in prayer!"

Did you love *Exploring The Psalms: Volume 2 - Exploring Key Elements*? Then you should read *Wisdom from a Watchman* by Jack Ferguson!

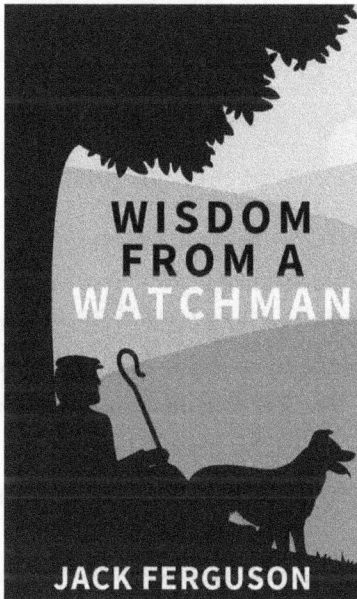

The late Jack Ferguson was known for being a "watchman on the walls", always alert to present or future dangers, challenges and opportunities for those that he pastored. This collection of some of his writings typifies his gentle, yet insightful ministry that is as perceptive now as it was when it was written.

Also by Hayes Press

Bible Studies
Bible Studies 1990 - First Samuel
Bible Studies 1991 - The First Letter of Paul to the Corinthians
Bible Studies 1993 - Second Samuel
Bible Studies 1994 - The Establishment and Development of
Churches of God
Bible Studies 1995 - The Kings of Judah and Israel from Solomon
to Asa
Bible Studies 1992 - The Second Letter of Paul to the Corinthians

Needed Truth
Needed Truth 1888
Needed Truth 2001
Needed Truth 2002
Needed Truth 2003
Needed Truth 2004
Needed Truth 2005
Needed Truth 2006
Needed Truth 2007

Needed Truth 2008
Needed Truth 2009
Needed Truth 2010
Needed Truth 2011
Needed Truth 2012
Needed Truth 2015
Needed Truth 1888-1988: A Centenary Review of Major Themes

Standalone
The Road Through Calvary: 40 Devotional Readings
Lovers of God's House
Different Discipleship: Jesus' Sermon on the Mount
The House of God: Past, Present and Future
The Kingdom of God
Knowing God: His Names and Nature
Churches of God: Their Biblical Constitution and Functions
Four Books About Jesus
Collected Writings On ... Exploring Biblical Fellowship
Collected Writings On ... Exploring Biblical Hope
Collected Writings On ... The Cross of Christ
Builders for God
Collected Writings On ... Exploring Biblical Faithfulness
Collected Writings On ... Exploring Biblical Joy
Possessing the Land: Spiritual Lessons from Joshua
Collected Writings On ... Exploring Biblical Holiness
Collected Writings On ... Exploring Biblical Faith
Collected Writings On ... Exploring Biblical Love
These Three Remain...Exploring Biblical Faith, Hope and Love
The Teaching and Testimony of the Apostles

Pressure Points - Biblical Advice for 20 of Life's Biggest Challenges

More Than a Saviour: Exploring the Person and Work of Jesus

The Psalms: Volumes 1-4 Boxset

The Faith: Outlines of Scripture Doctrine

Key Doctrines of the Christian Gospel

Is There a Purpose to Life?

An Introduction to Bible Covenants

The Hidden Christ - Volume 2: Types and Shadows in Offerings and Sacrifices

The Hidden Christ Volume 1: Types and Shadows in the Old Testament

The Hidden Christ - Volume 3: Types and Shadows in Genesis

Heavenly Meanings - The Parables of Jesus

Fisherman to Follower: The Life and Teaching of Simon Peter

Called to Serve: Lessons from the Levites

Needed Truth 2017 Issue 1

The Breaking of the Bread: Its History, Its Observance, Its Meaning

Spiritual Revivals of the Bible

An Introduction to the Book of Hebrews

The Holy Spirit and the Believer

Exploring The Psalms: Volume 1 - Thoughts on Key Themes

Exploring The Psalms: Volume 2 - Exploring Key Elements

The Psalms: Volume 3 - Surveying Key Sections

The Psalms: Volume 4 - Savouring Choice Selections

Profiles of the Prophets

The Hidden Christ - Volumes 1-4 Box Set

The Hidden Christ - Volume 4: Types and Shadows in Israel's Tabernacle

Baptism - Its Meaning and Teaching

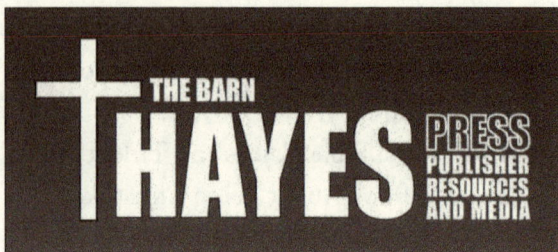

About the Publisher

Hayes Press (www.hayespress.org) is a registered charity in the United Kingdom, whose primary mission is to disseminate the Word of God, mainly through literature. It is one of the largest distributors of gospel tracts and leaflets in the United Kingdom, with over 100 titles and hundreds of thousands despatched annually. In addition to paperbacks and eBooks, Hayes Press also publishes Plus Eagles Wings, a fun and educational Bible magazine for children, and Golden Bells, a popular daily Bible reading calendar in wall or desk formats. Also available are over 100 Bibles in many different versions, shapes and sizes, Bible text posters and much more!

www.ingramcontent.com/pod-product-compliance
Lightning Source LLC
Chambersburg PA
CBHW021207020426
42331CB00003B/253